Alice in Wonderland

ADULT COLORING BOOK

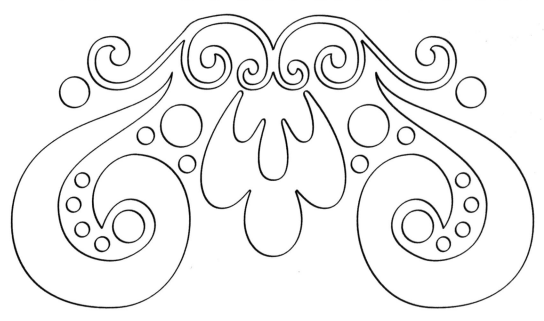

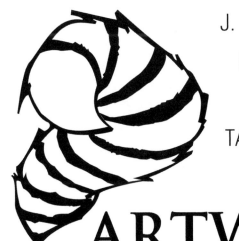

J. SCOTT CAMPBELL

DANIEL LEISTER

RICHARD ORTIZ

TALENT CALDWELL

RICH BONK

ARTWORK BY:

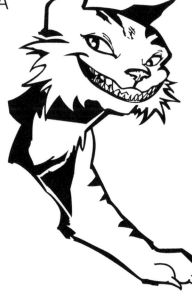

DAVID NAKAYAMA

SEAN CHEN

CHRIS EHNOT

ANTHONY SPAY

JASON METCALF

AL RIO

MIKE KROME

NOAH SALONGA

ADRIANA MELO

PRODUCTION & DESIGN: CHRISTOPHER COTE & ASHLEY VANACORE
MANAGING EDITOR: JENNIFER BERMEL

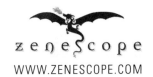

WWW.ZENESCOPE.COM

Joe Brusha President & Chief Creative Officer
Christopher Cote Art Director
Pat Shand Writer & Editor
Dave Franchini Assistant Editor
Jessica Rossana Assistant Editor
Joi Dariel Production Manager

John Lyons Director of Sales & Marketing
Jennifer Bermel Director of Business Development
Jason Condeelis Direct Market Sales & Customer Service
Stu Kropnick Operations Manager
Ralph Tedesco VP Film & Television

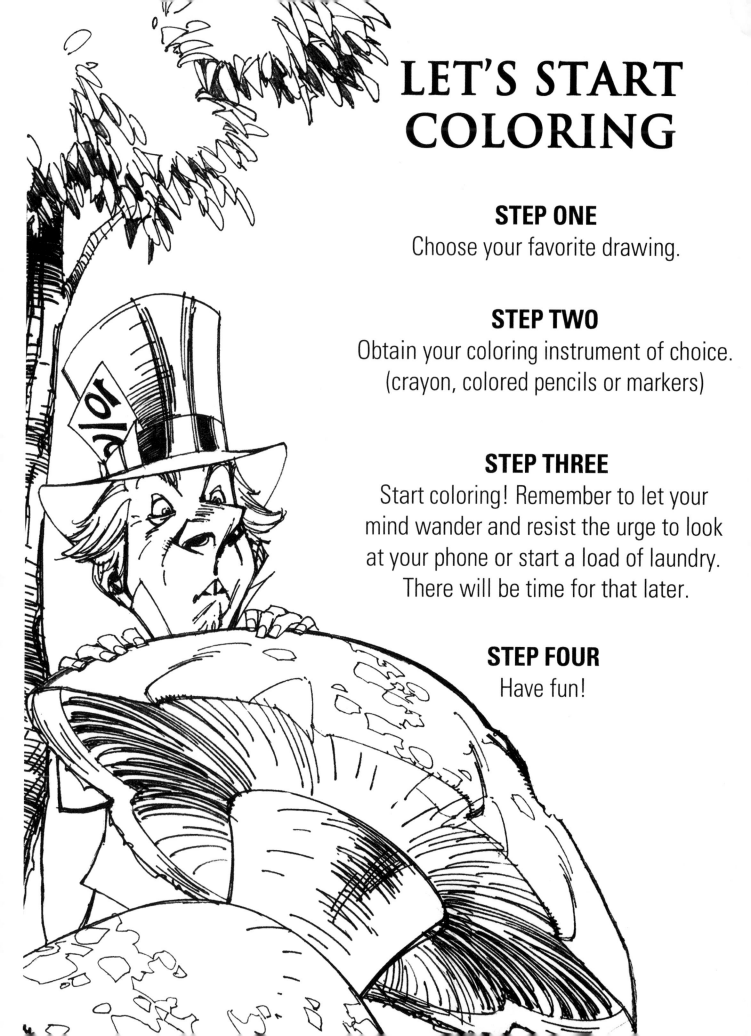

LET'S START COLORING

STEP ONE
Choose your favorite drawing.

STEP TWO
Obtain your coloring instrument of choice.
(crayon, colored pencils or markers)

STEP THREE
Start coloring! Remember to let your
mind wander and resist the urge to look
at your phone or start a load of laundry.
There will be time for that later.

STEP FOUR
Have fun!

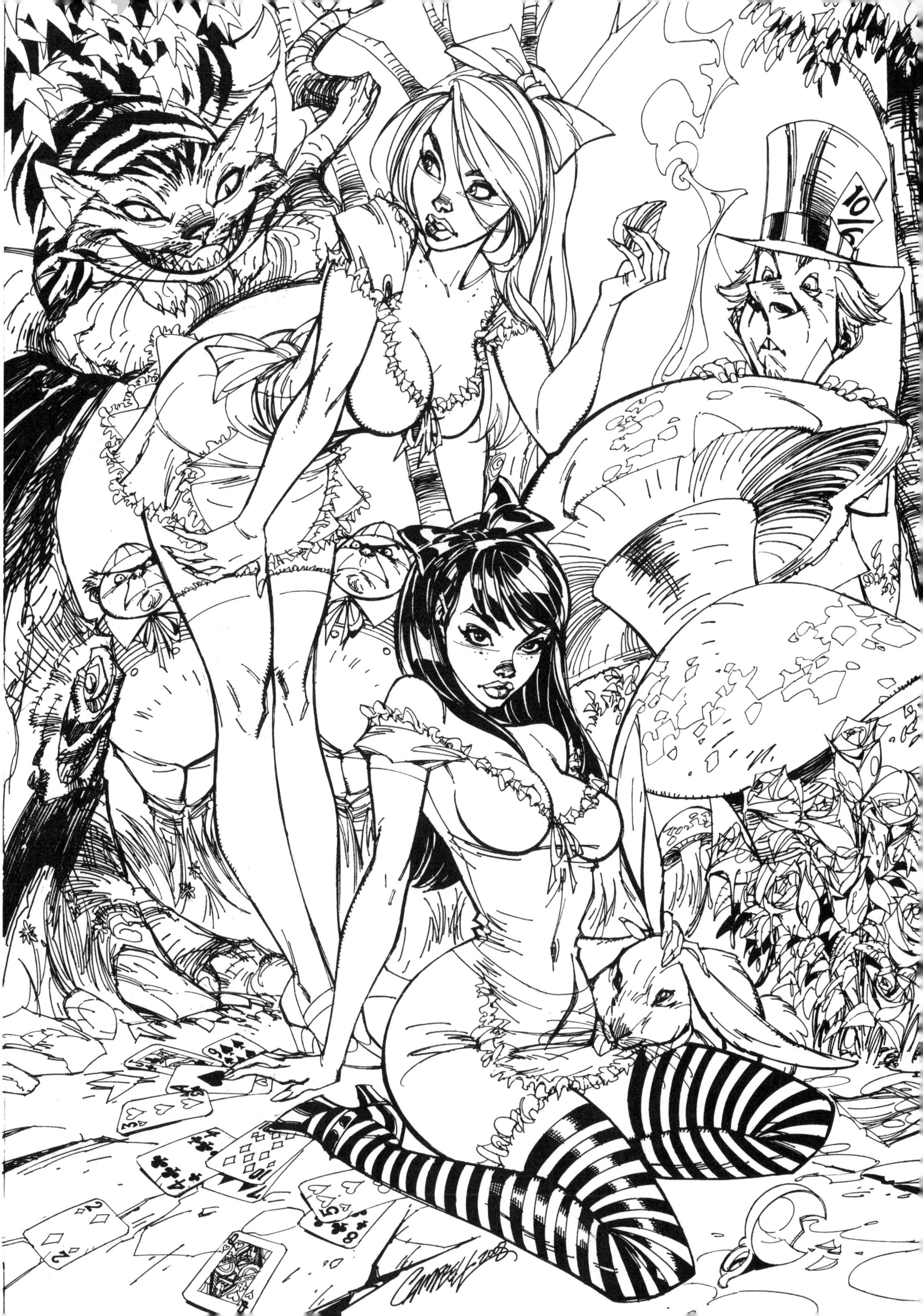
10/6

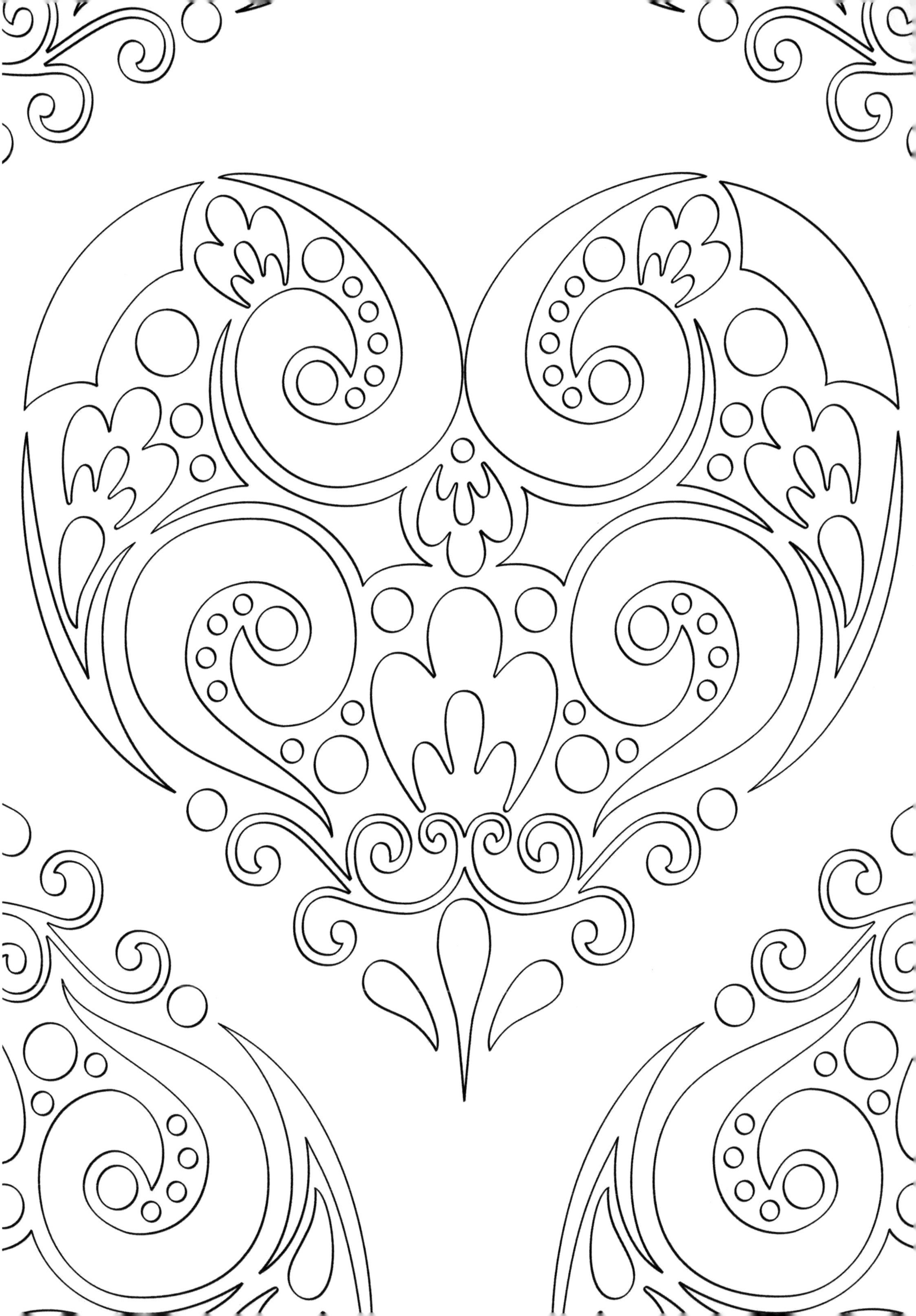

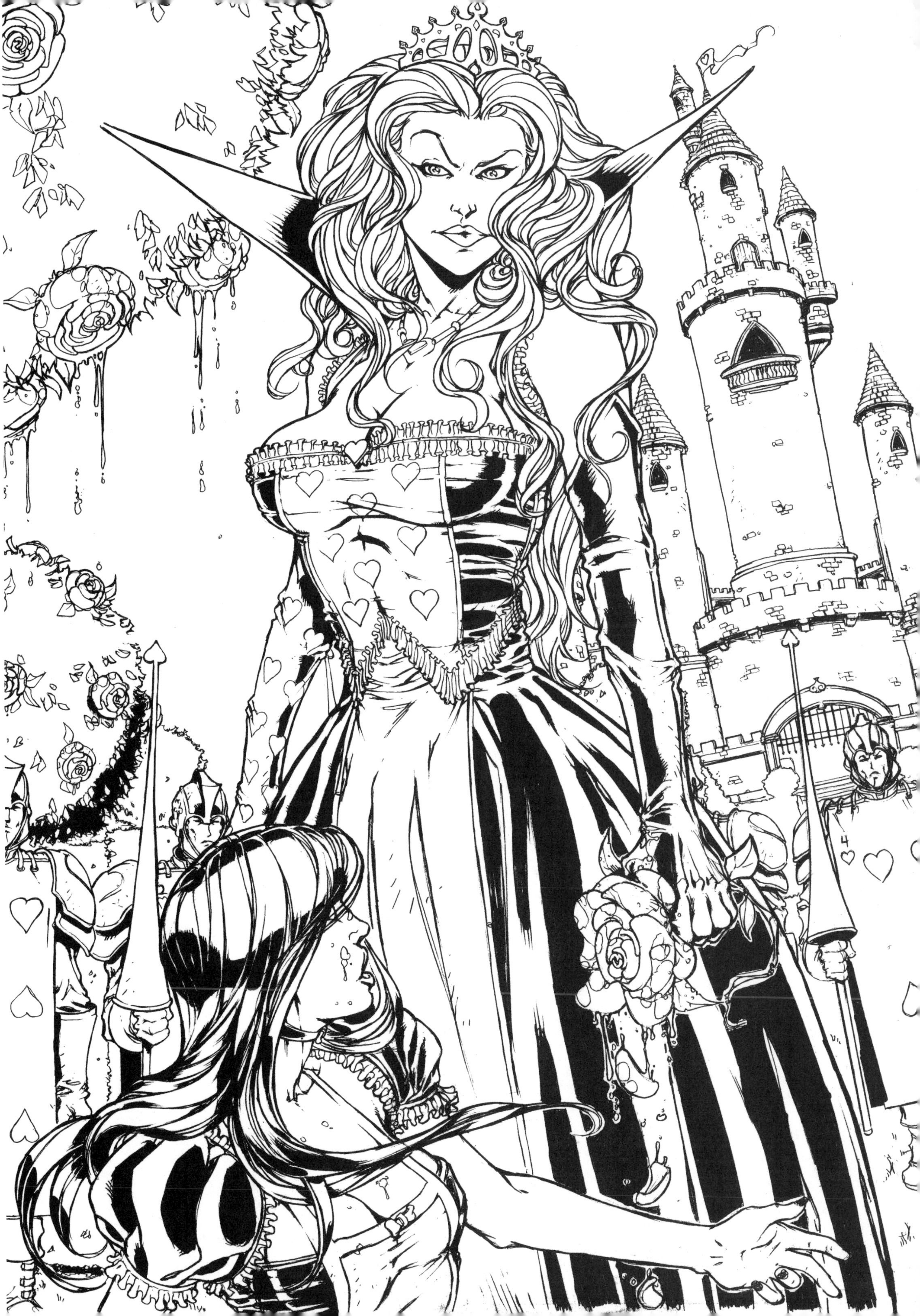

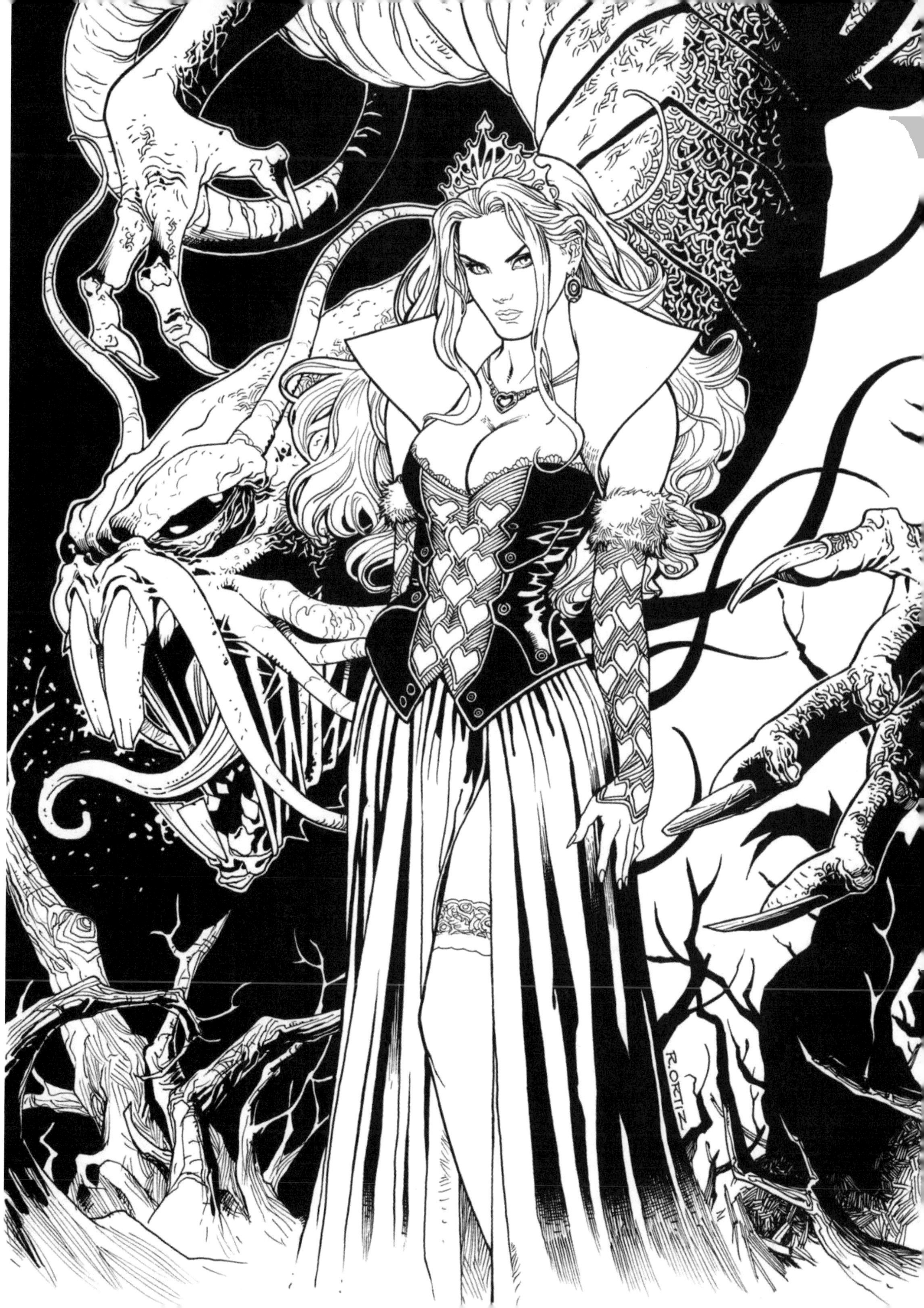
R. ORTIZ

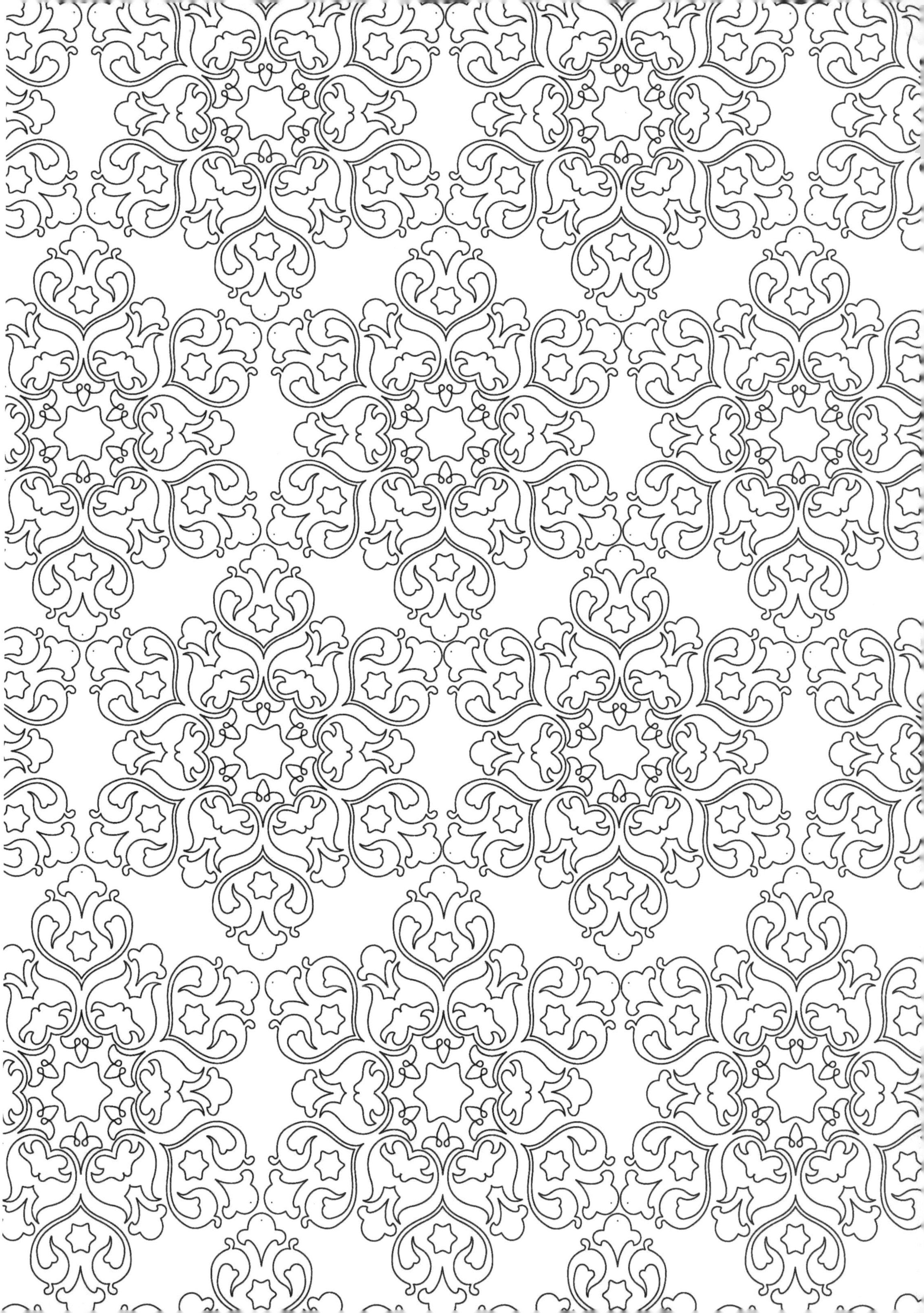

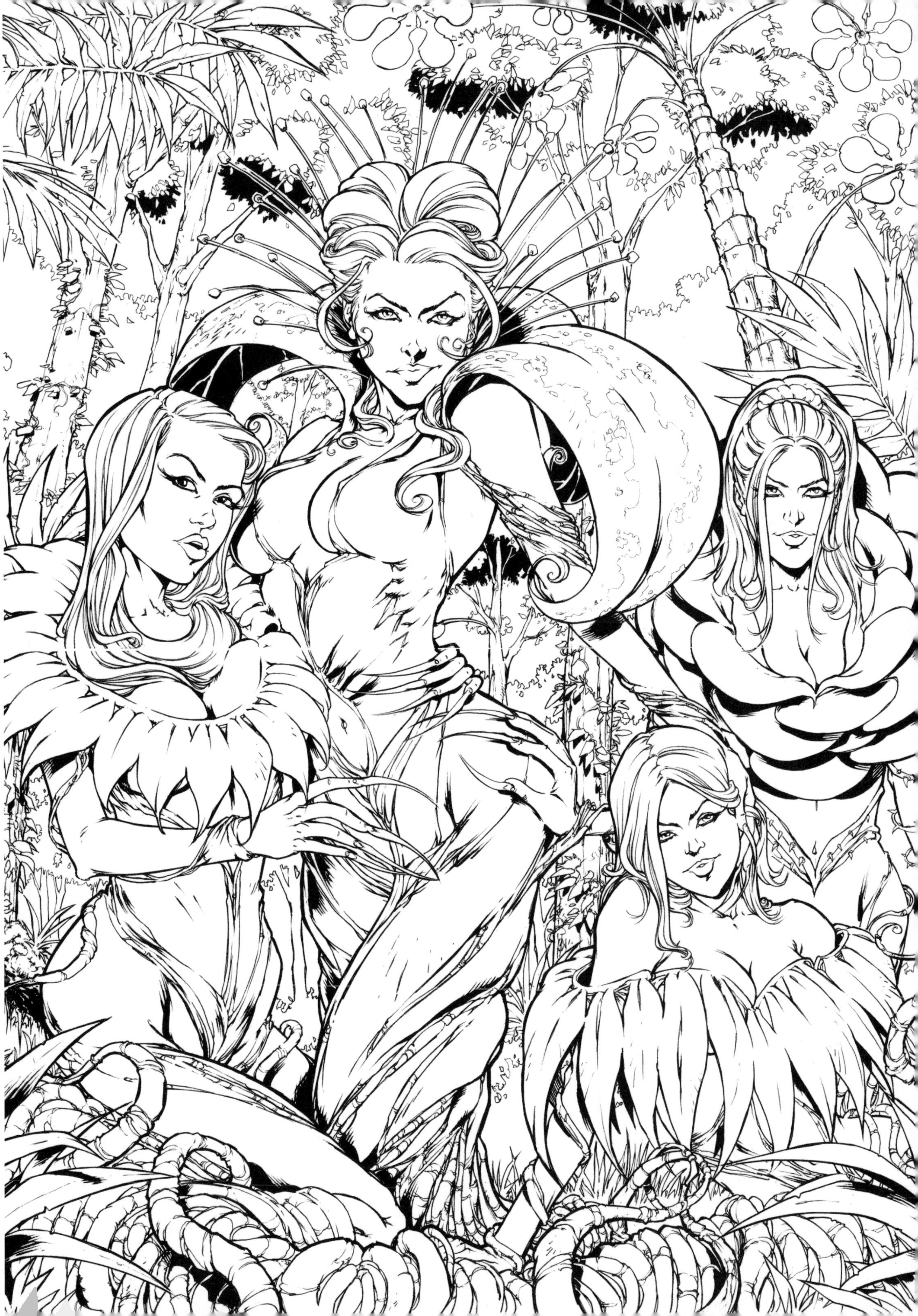

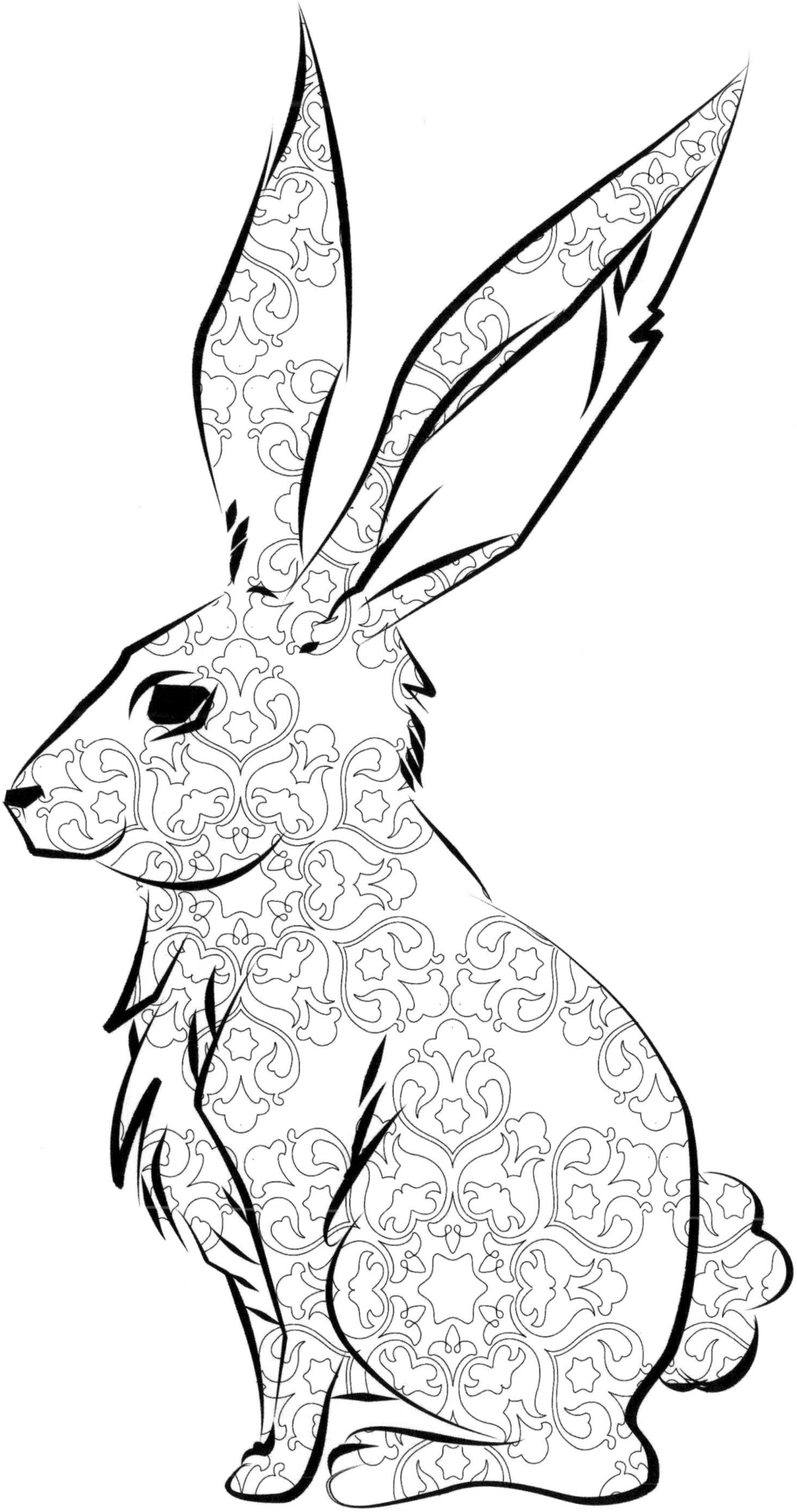

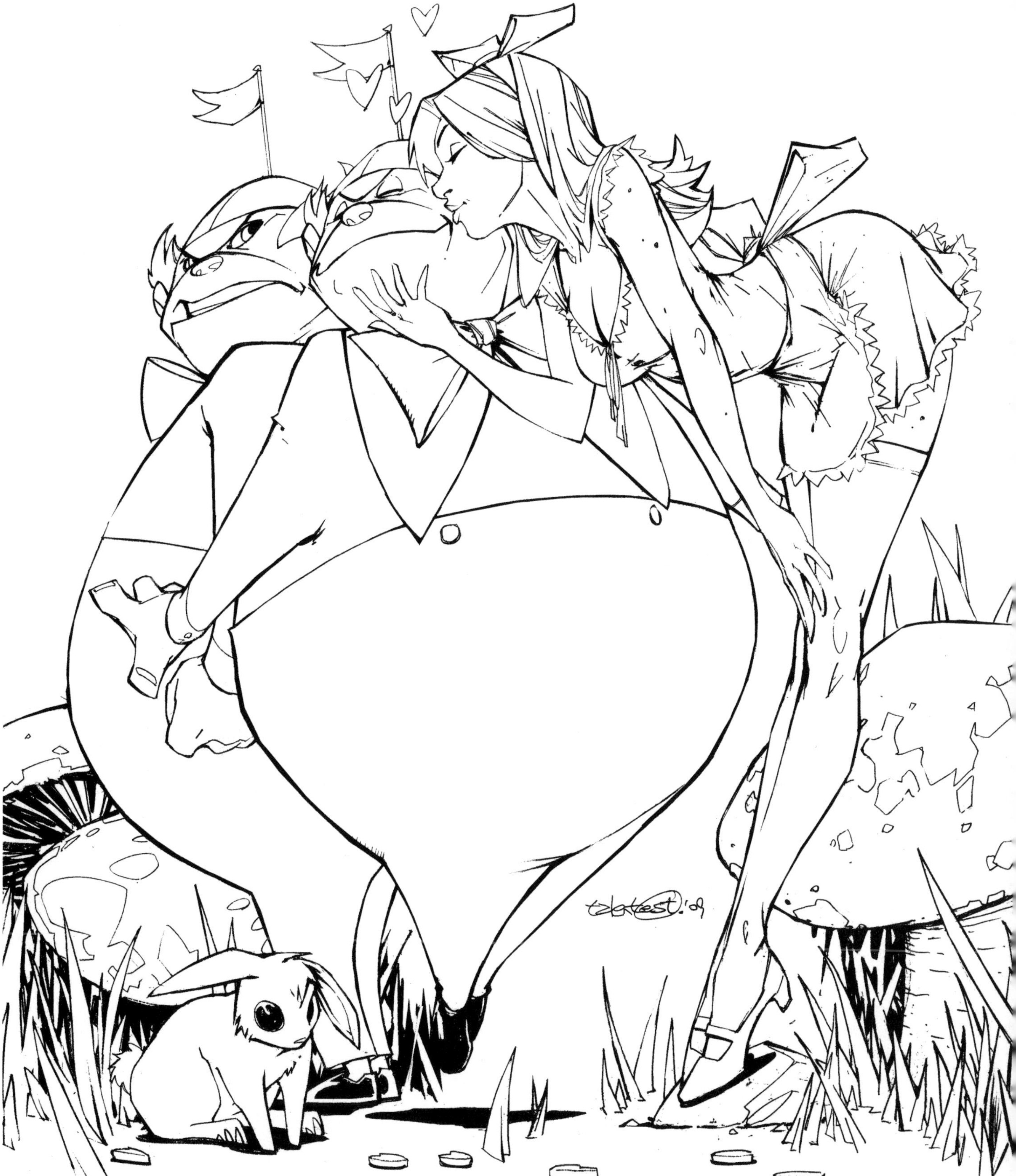

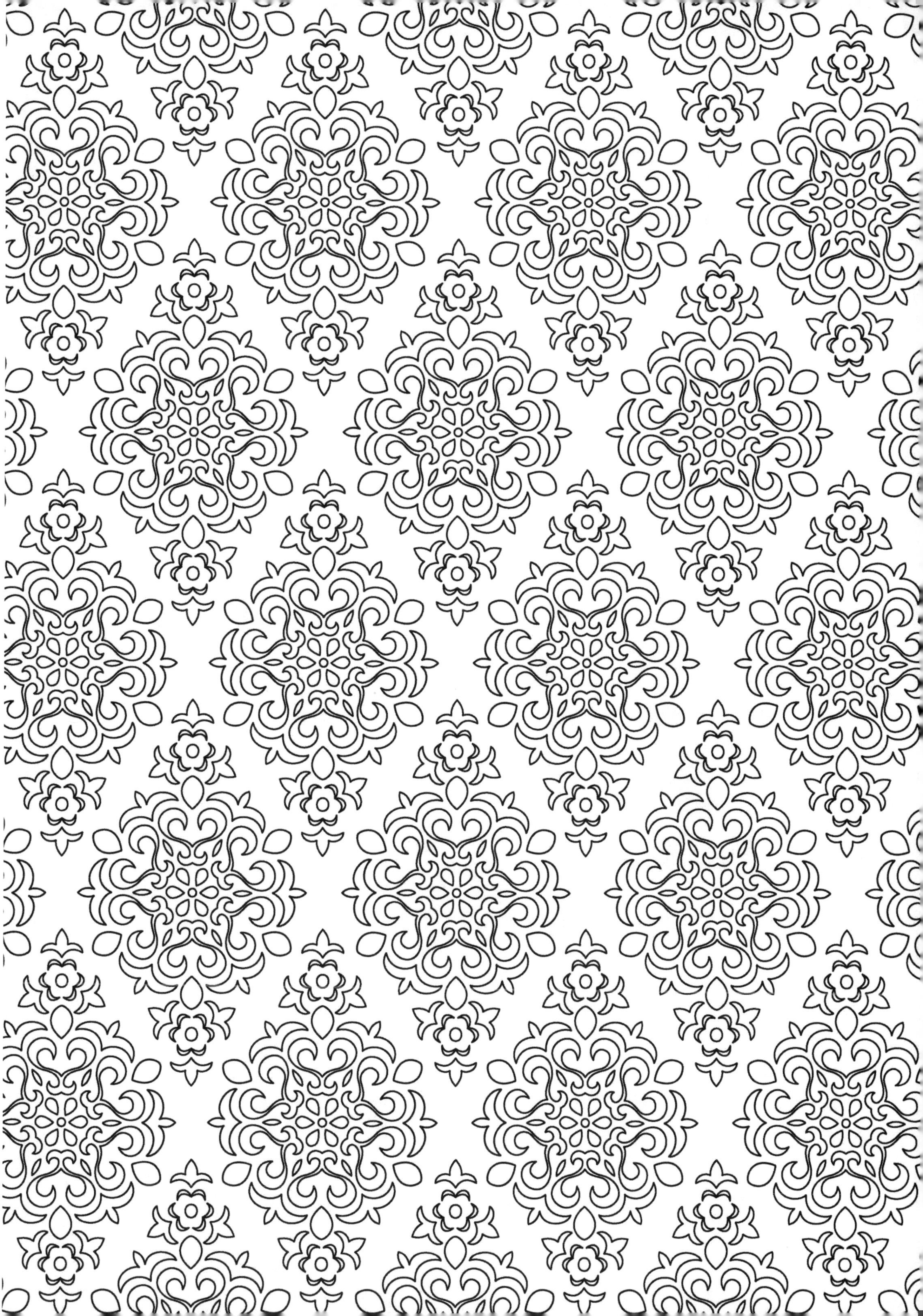

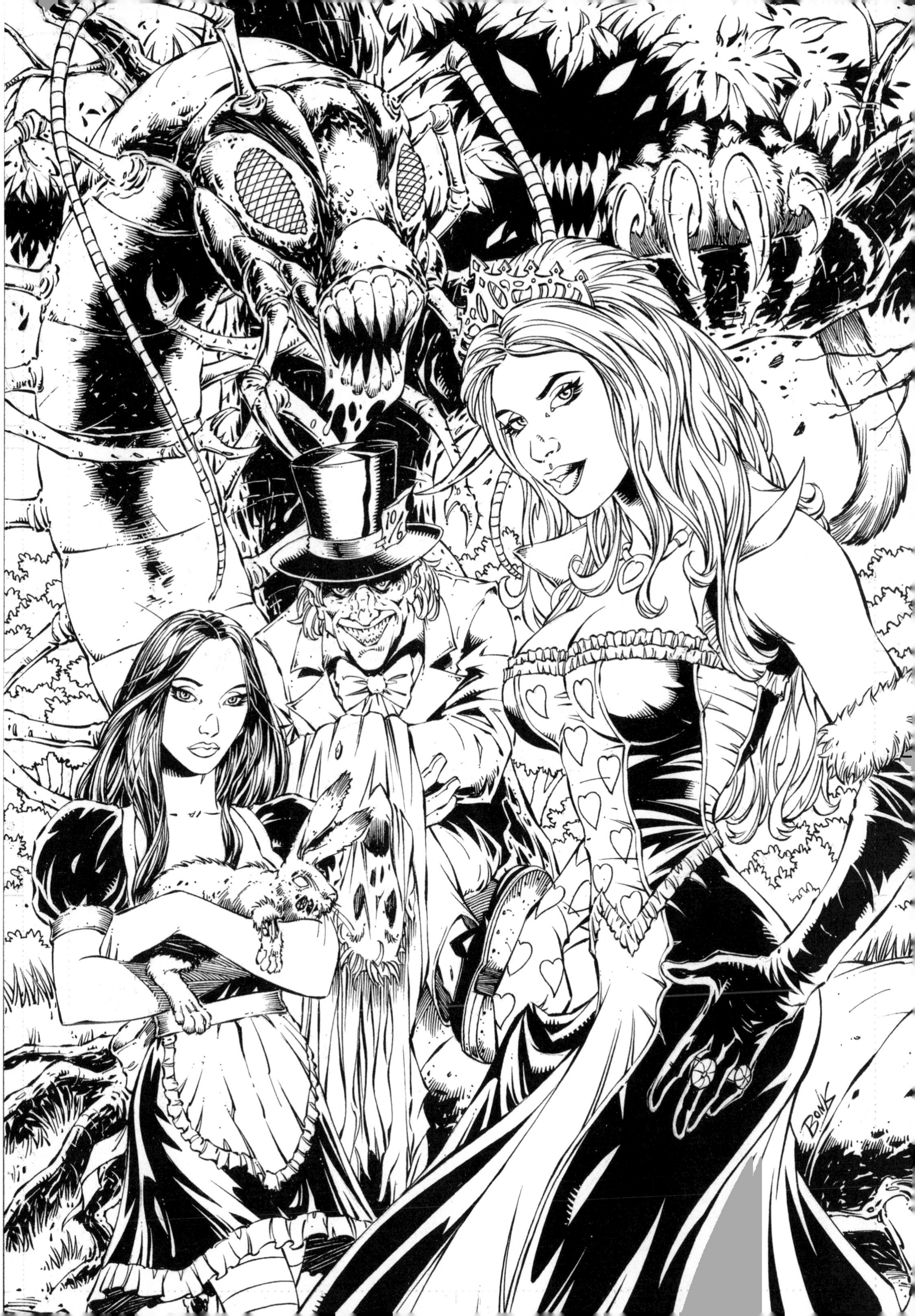

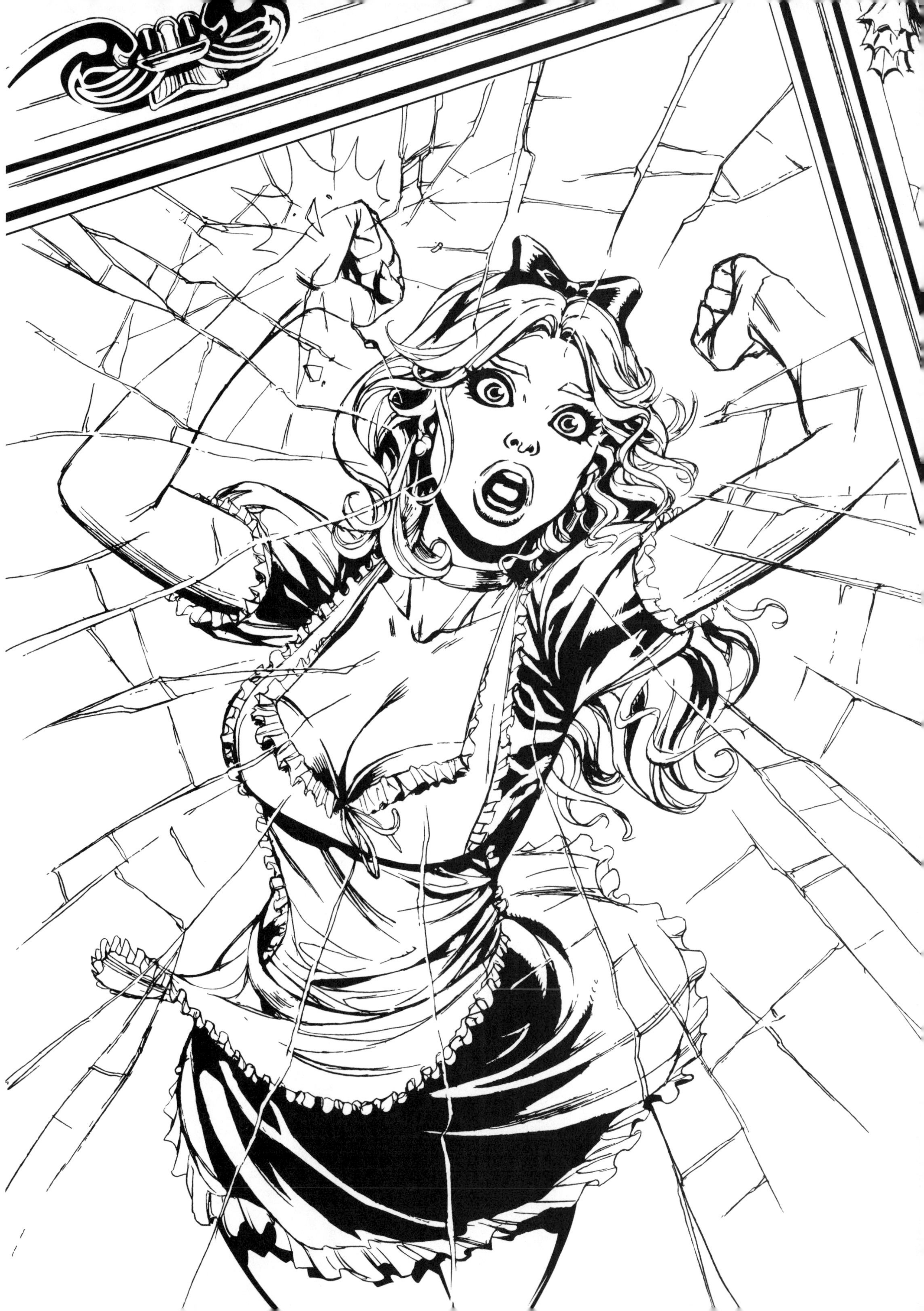

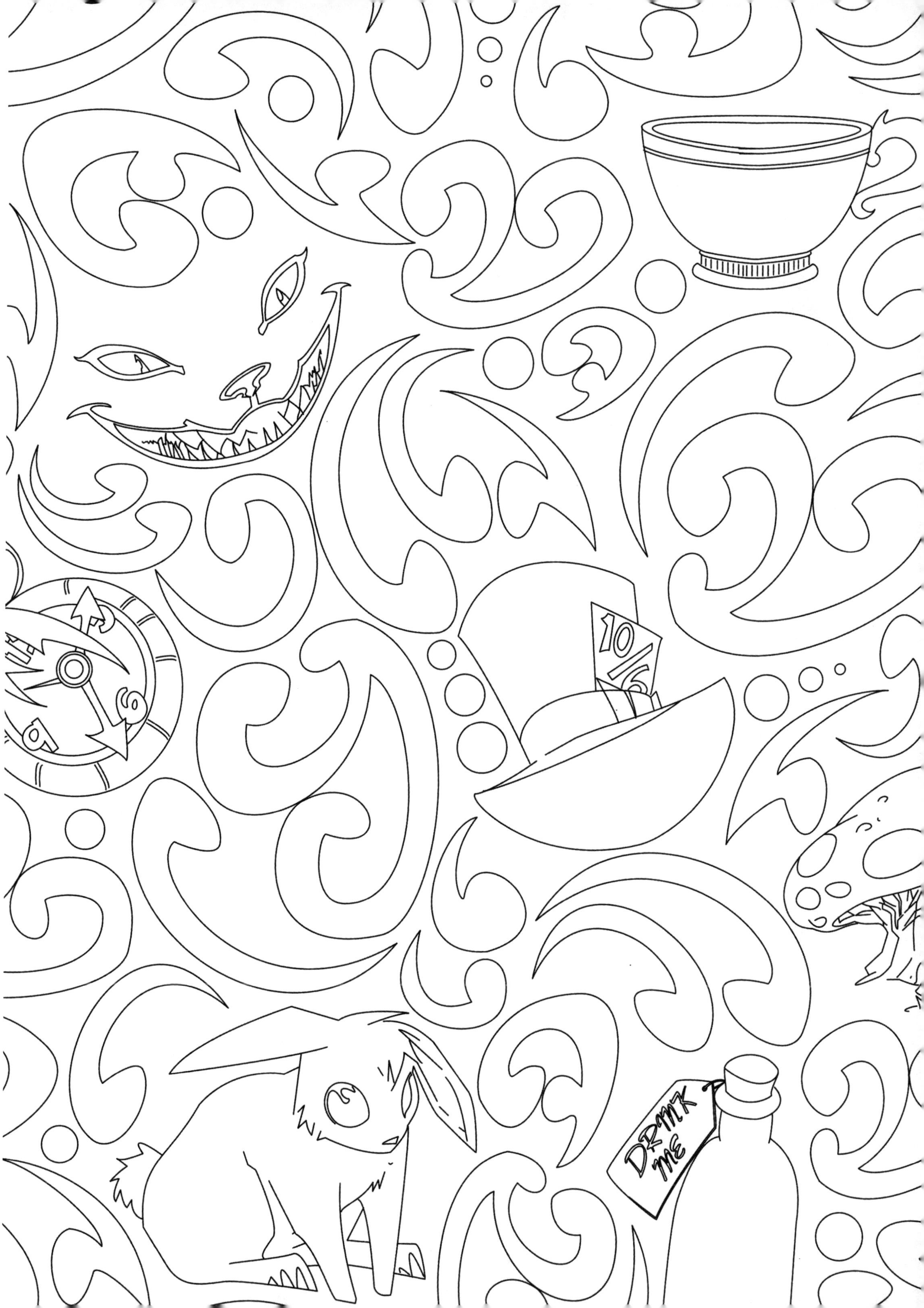
10/6
DRINK ME

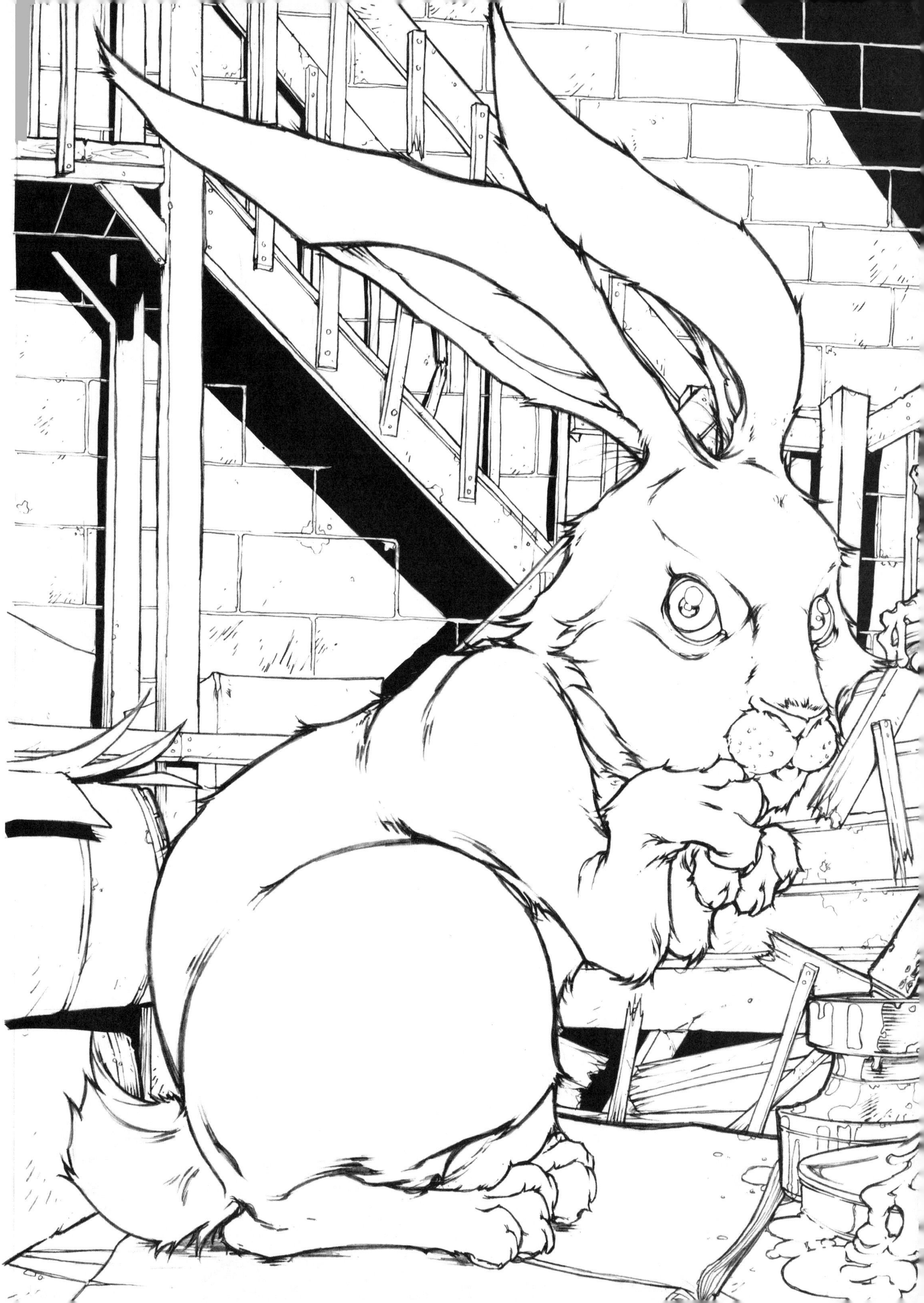

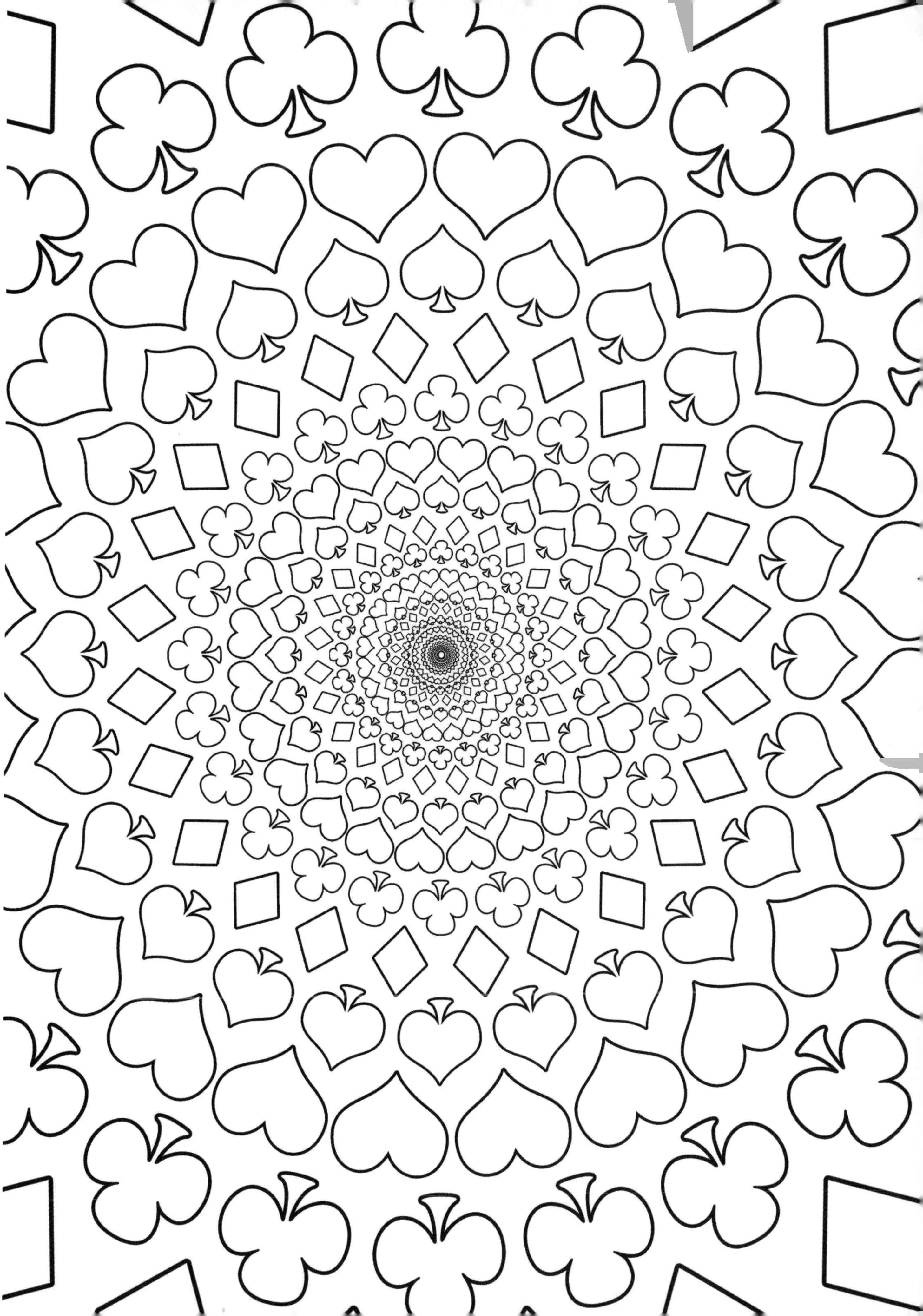

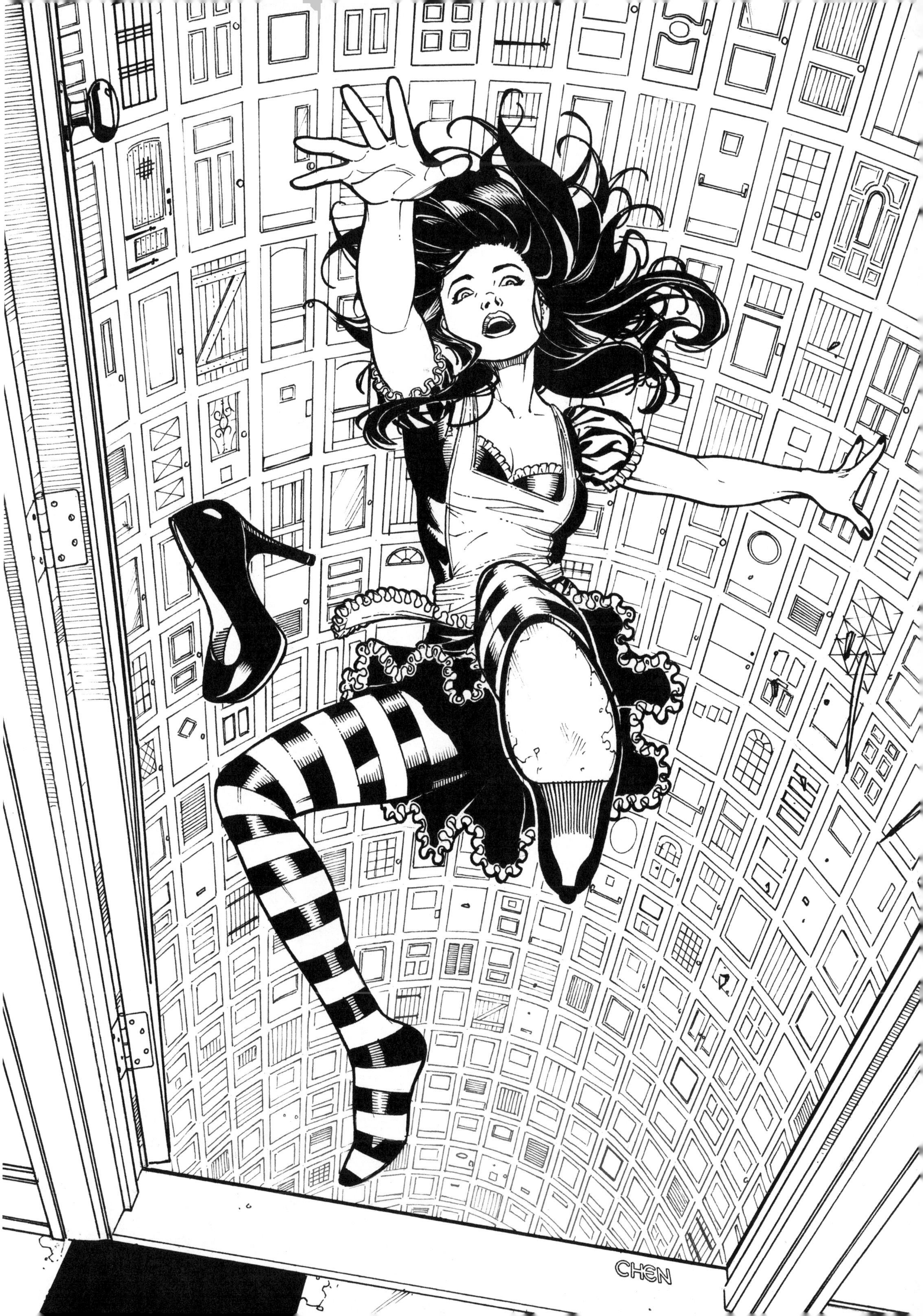
CHEN

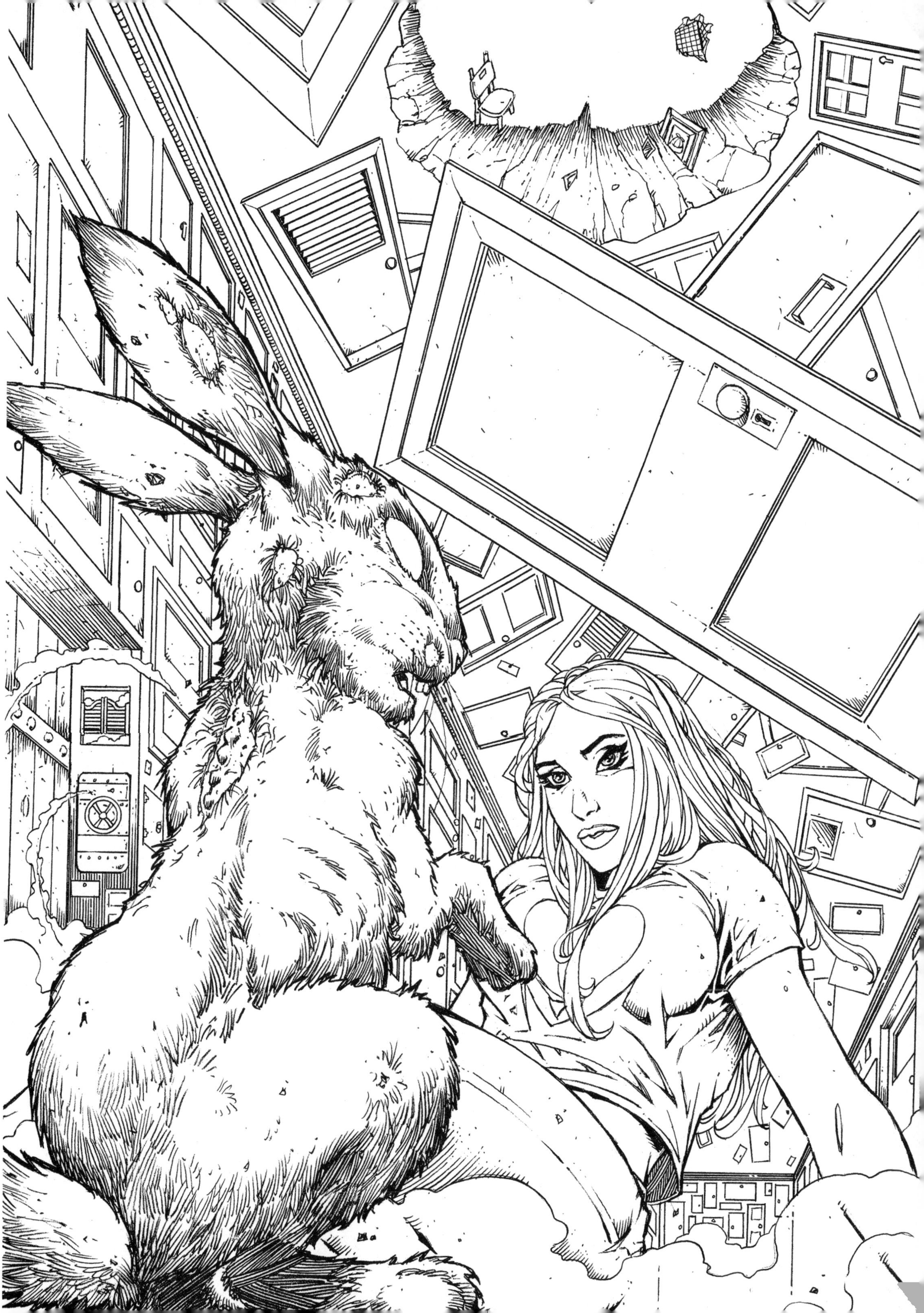

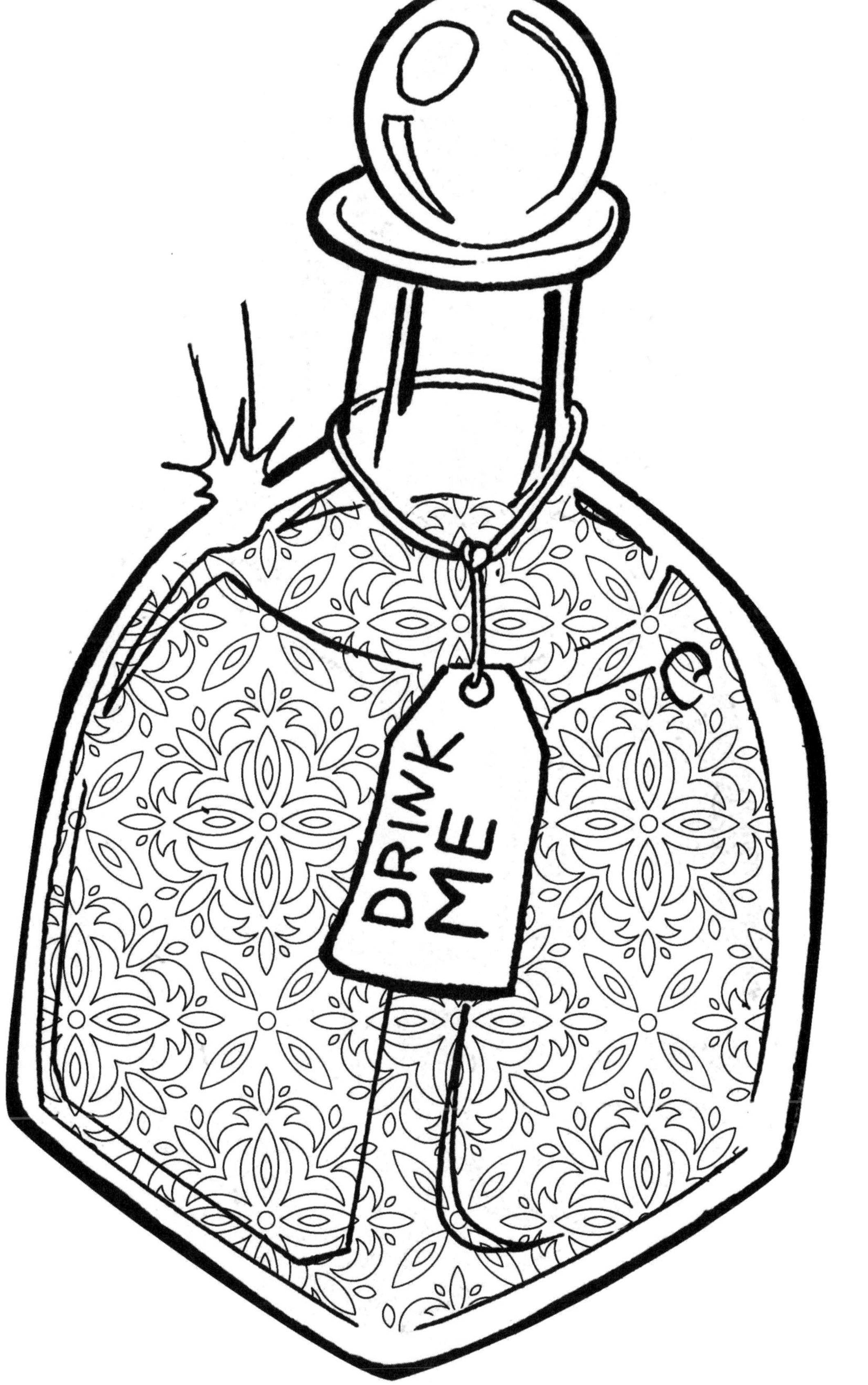
DRINK
ME

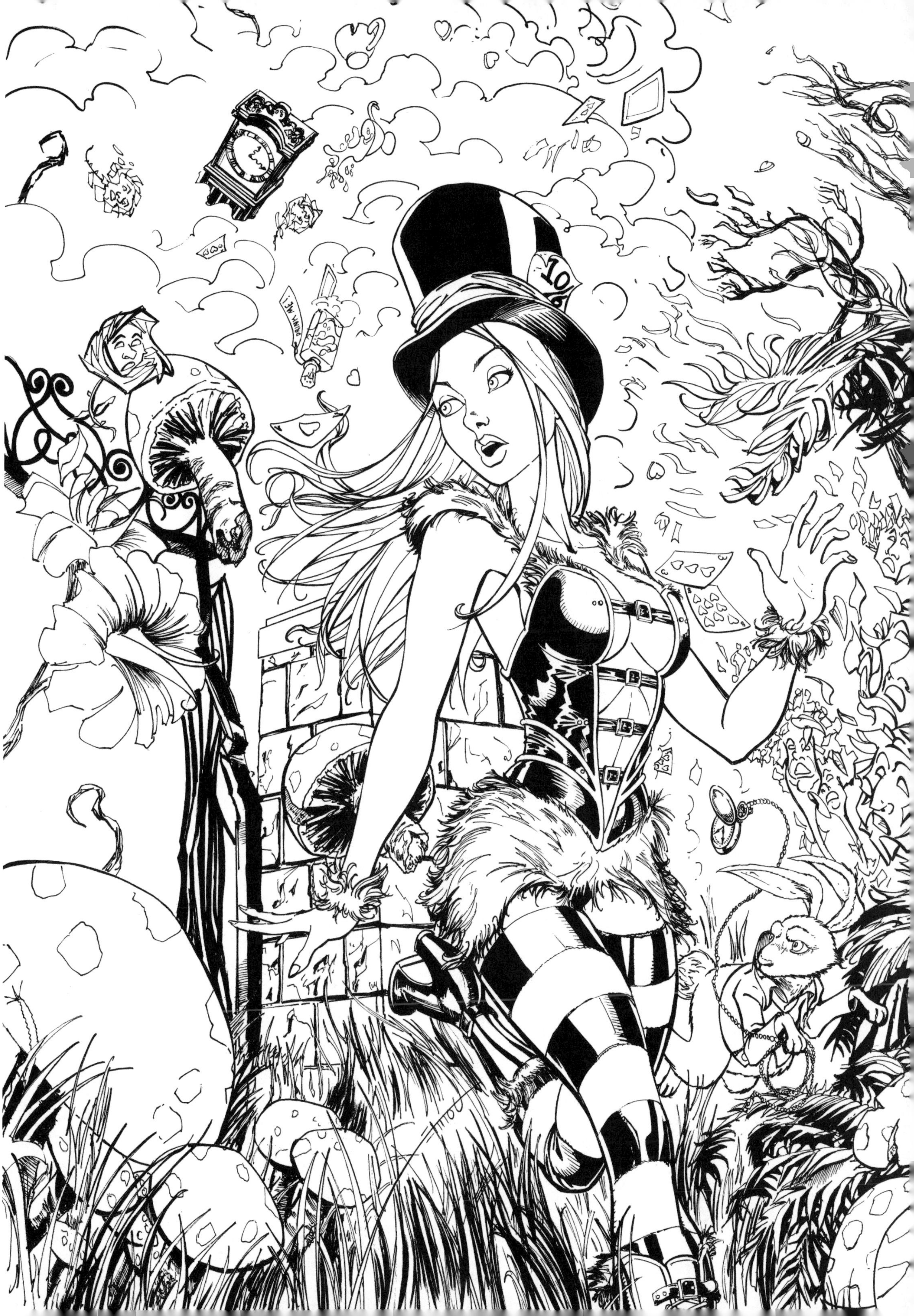

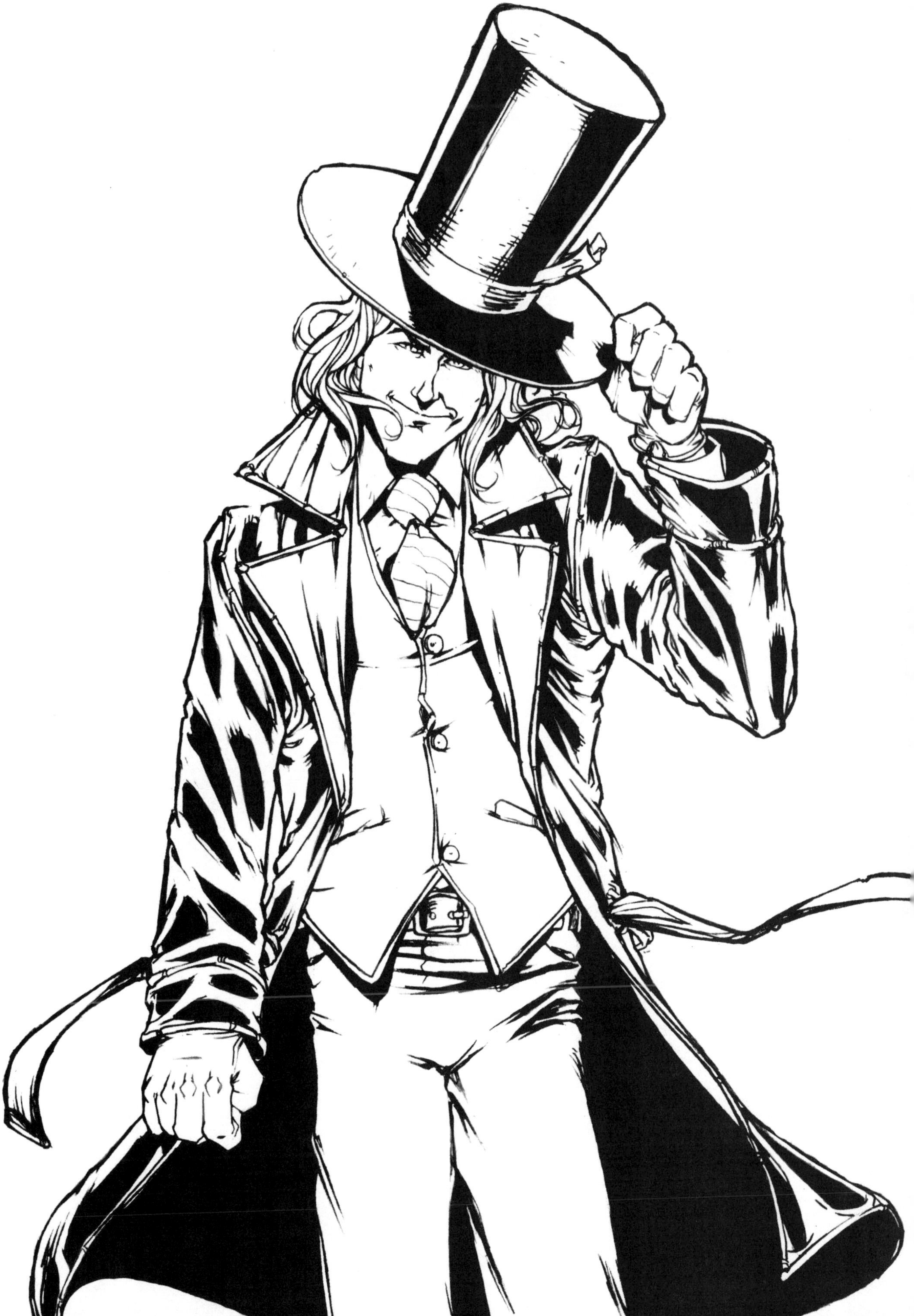

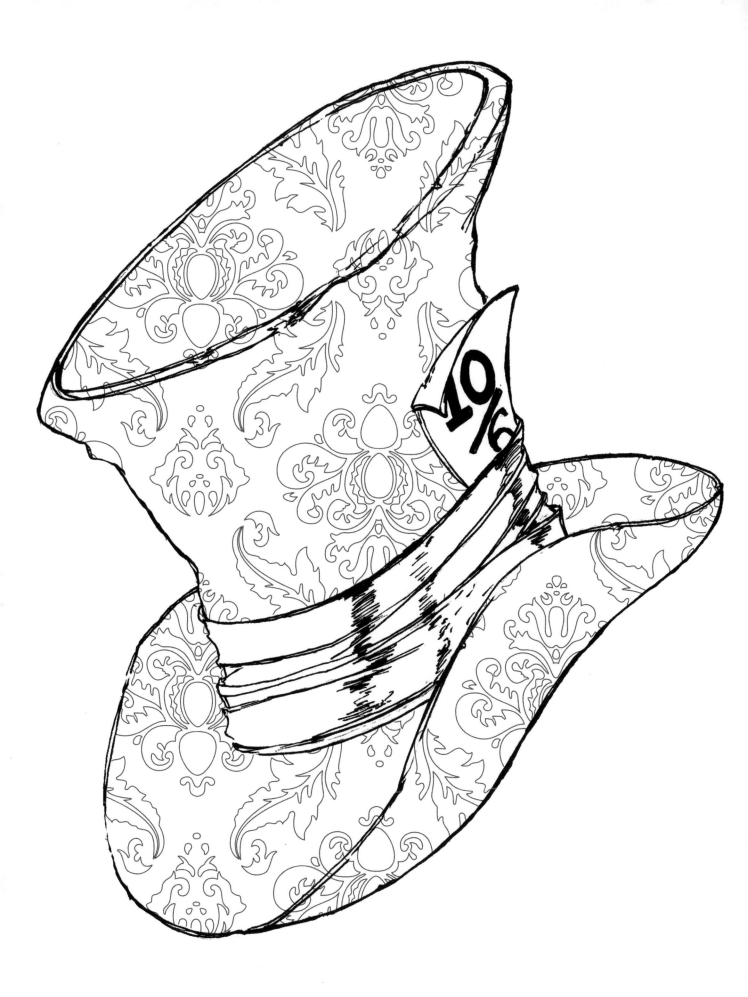

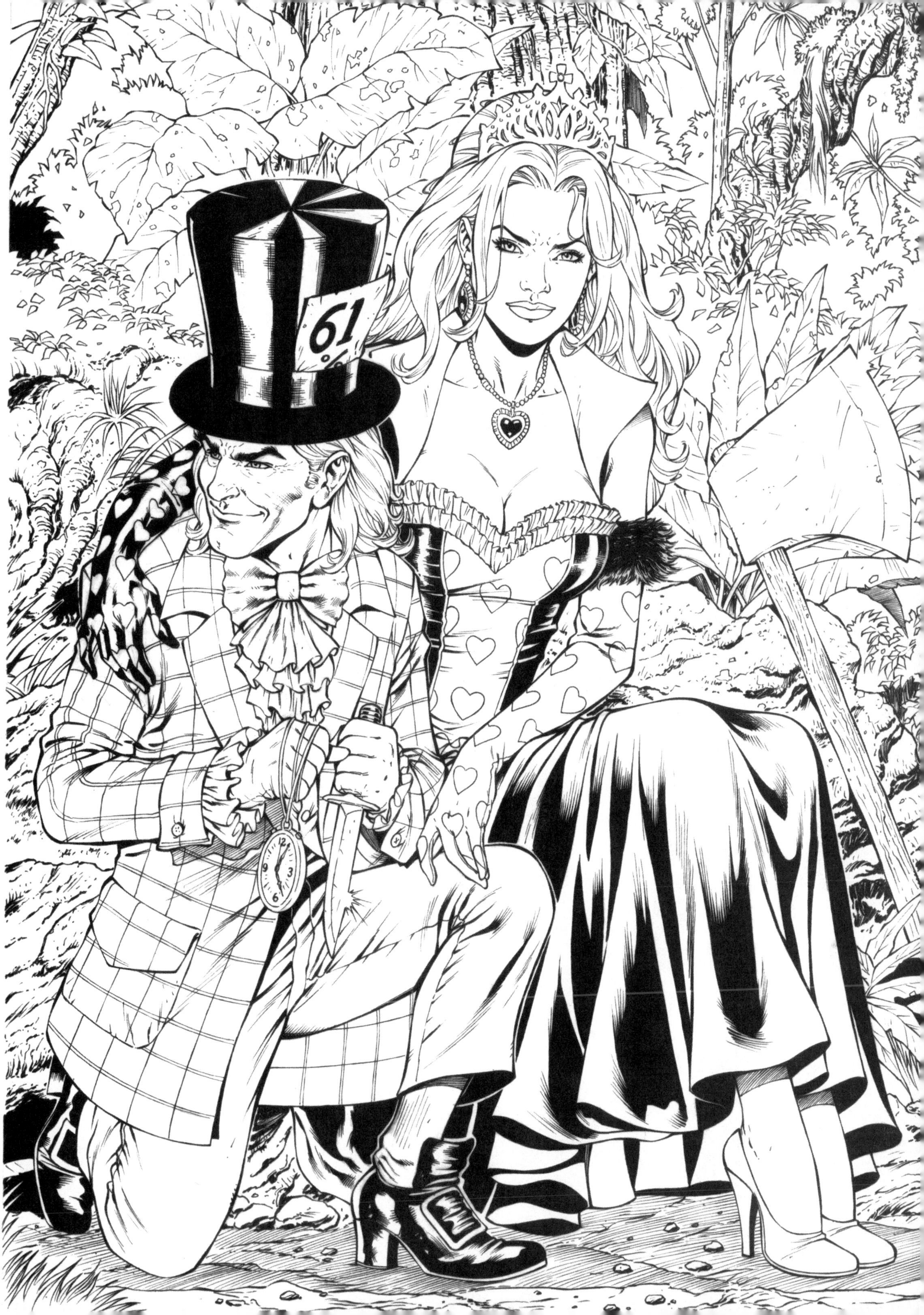
61

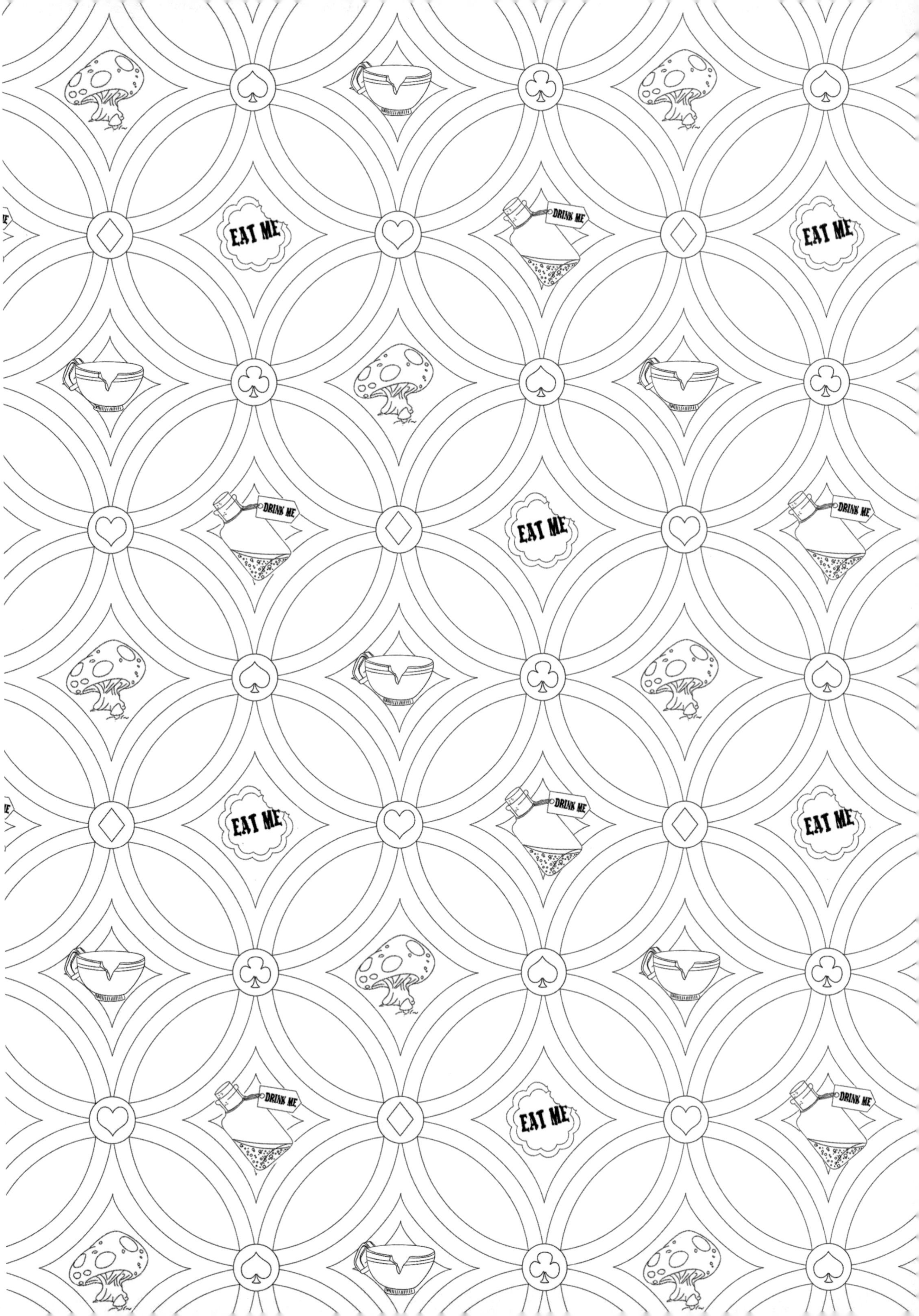
EAT ME
DRINK ME
EAT ME
DRINK ME
EAT ME
DRINK ME
EAT ME
DRINK ME
EAT ME
DRINK ME
EAT ME
DRINK ME

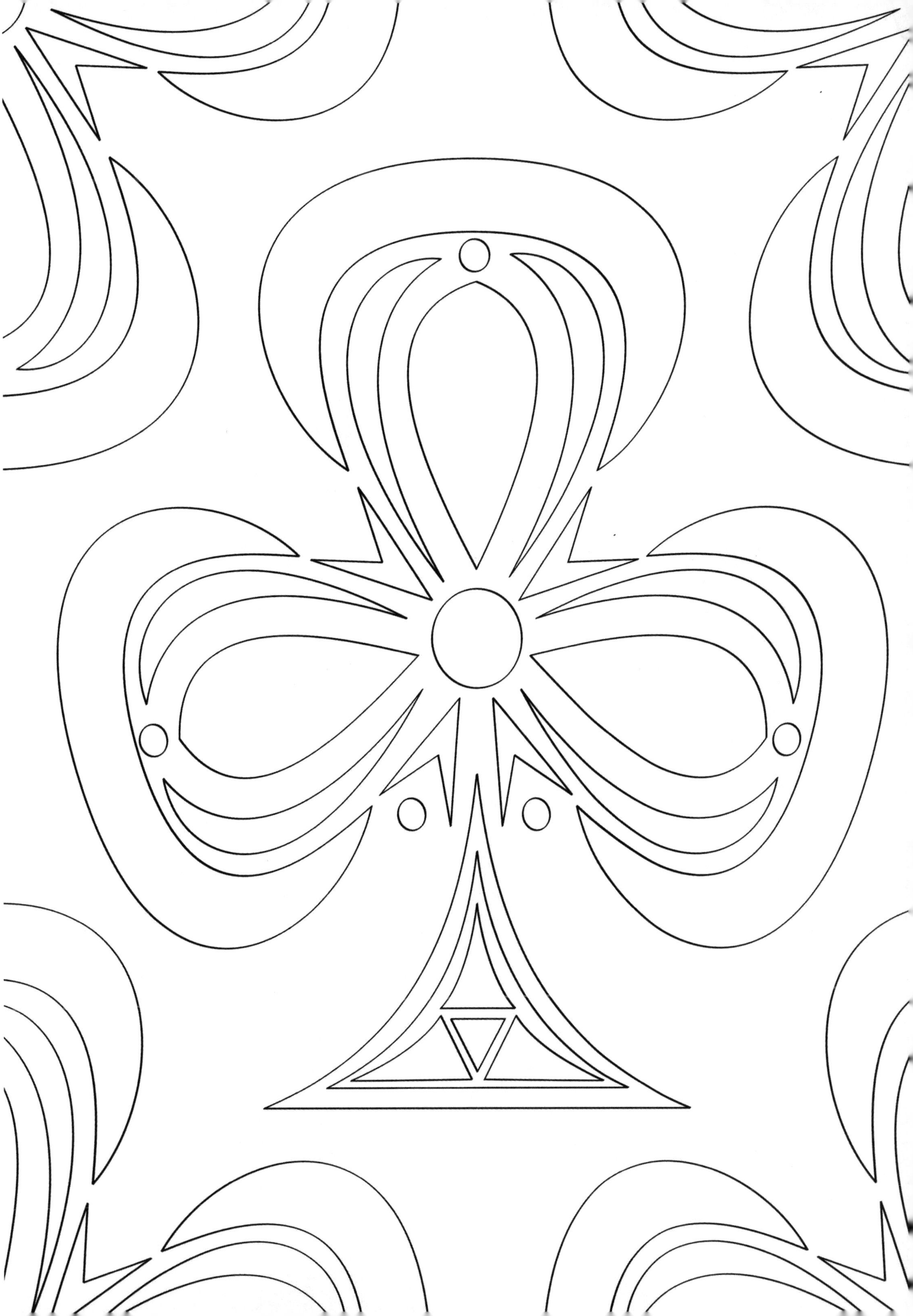

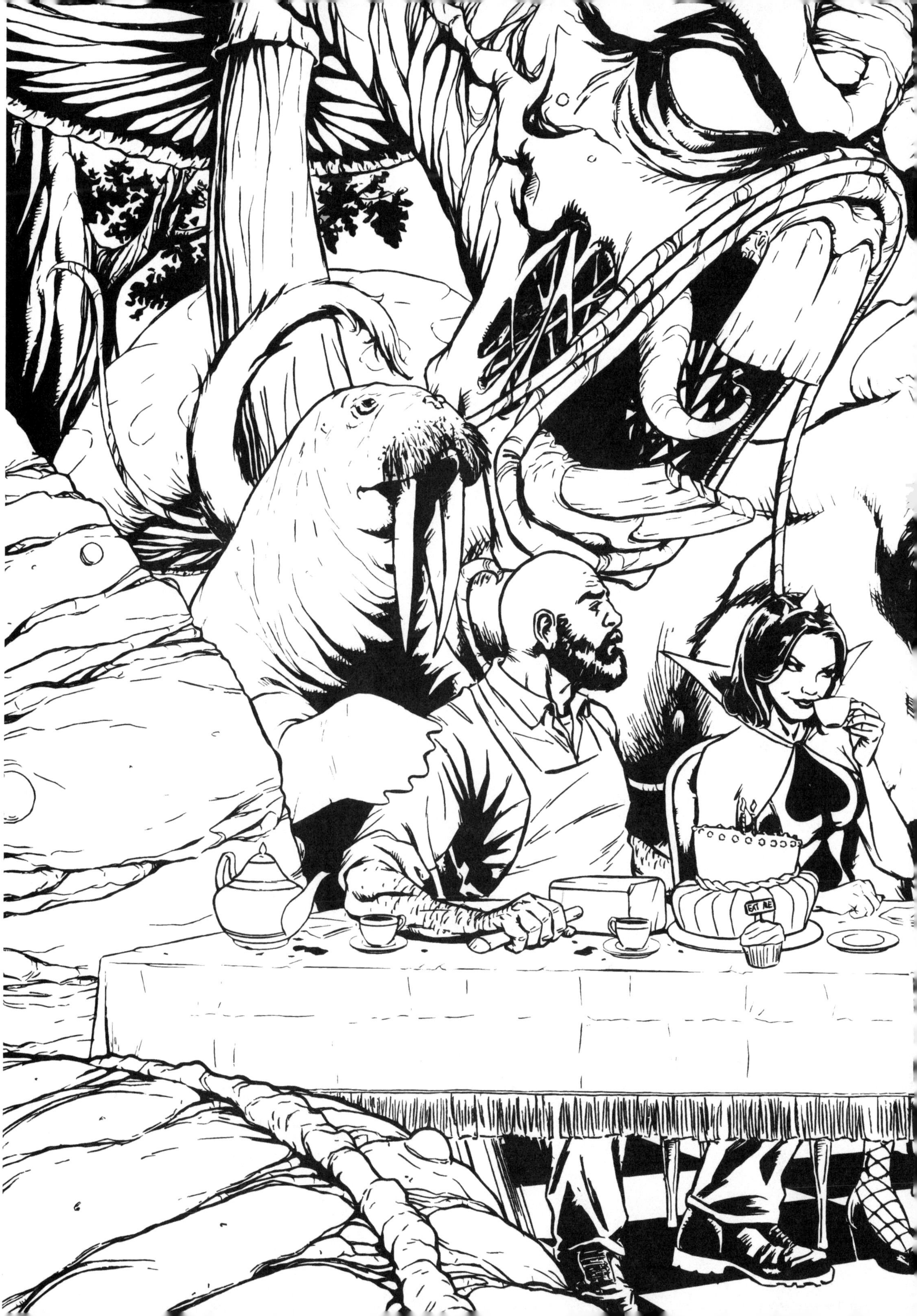
EAT ME

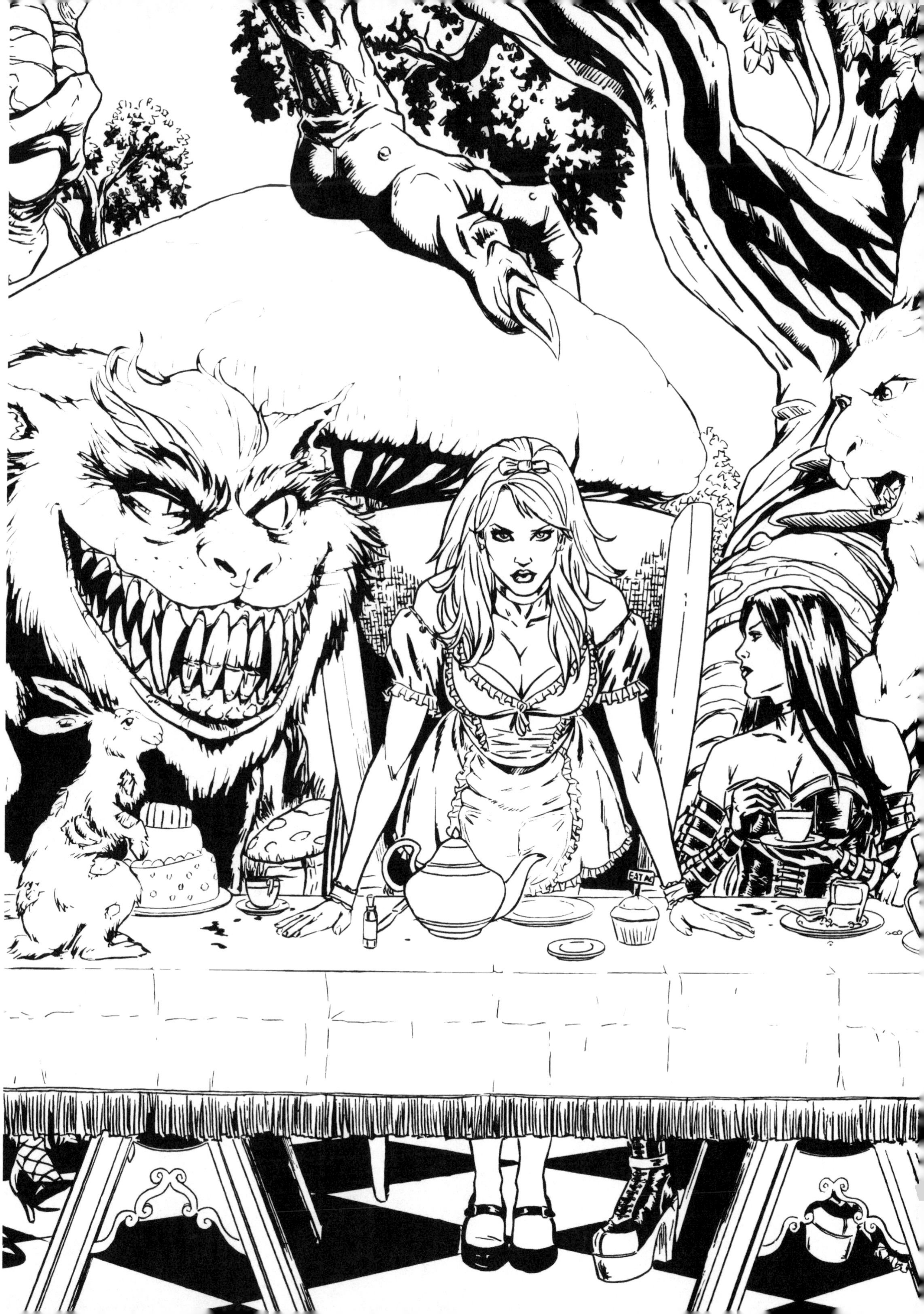

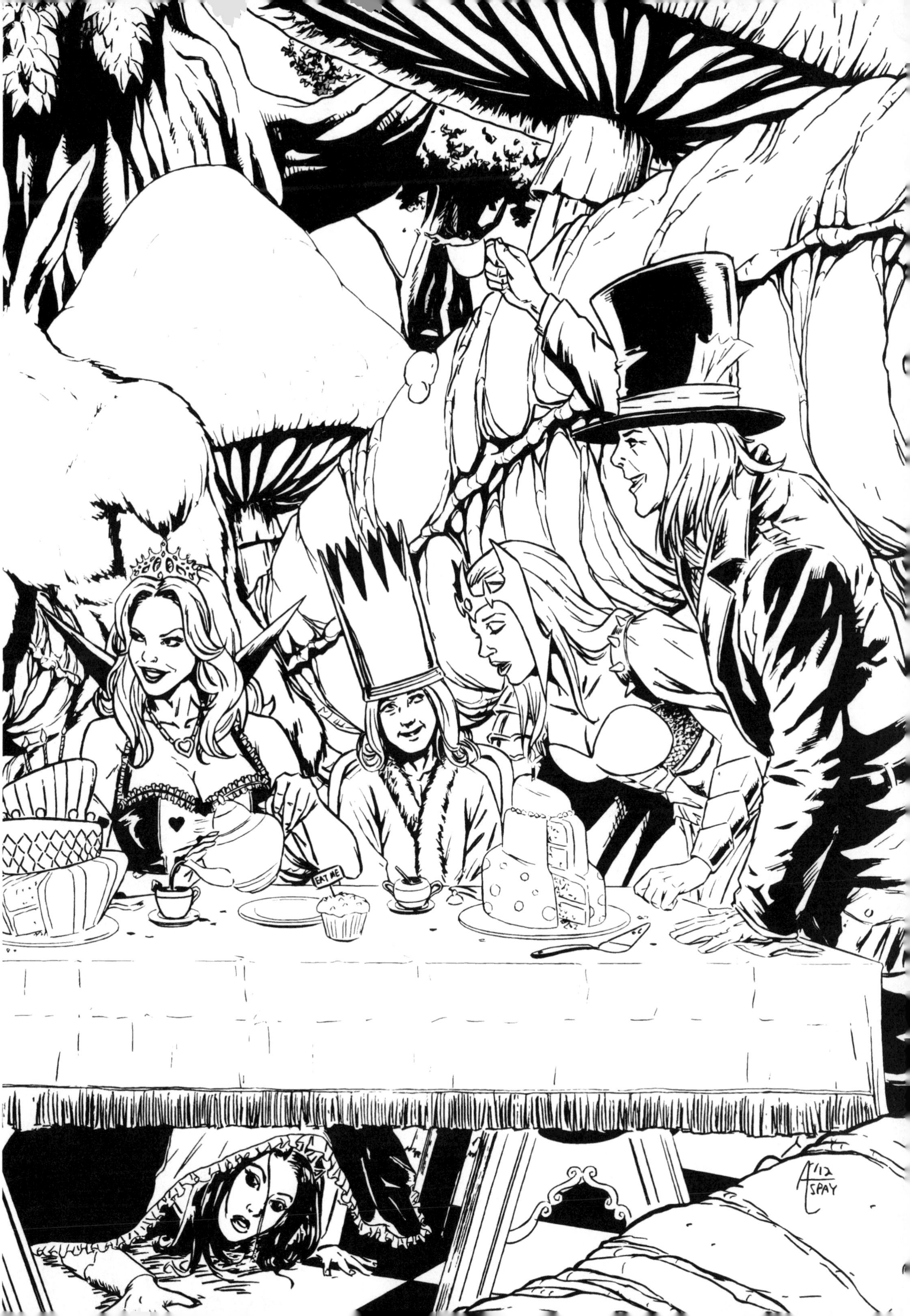
EAT ME

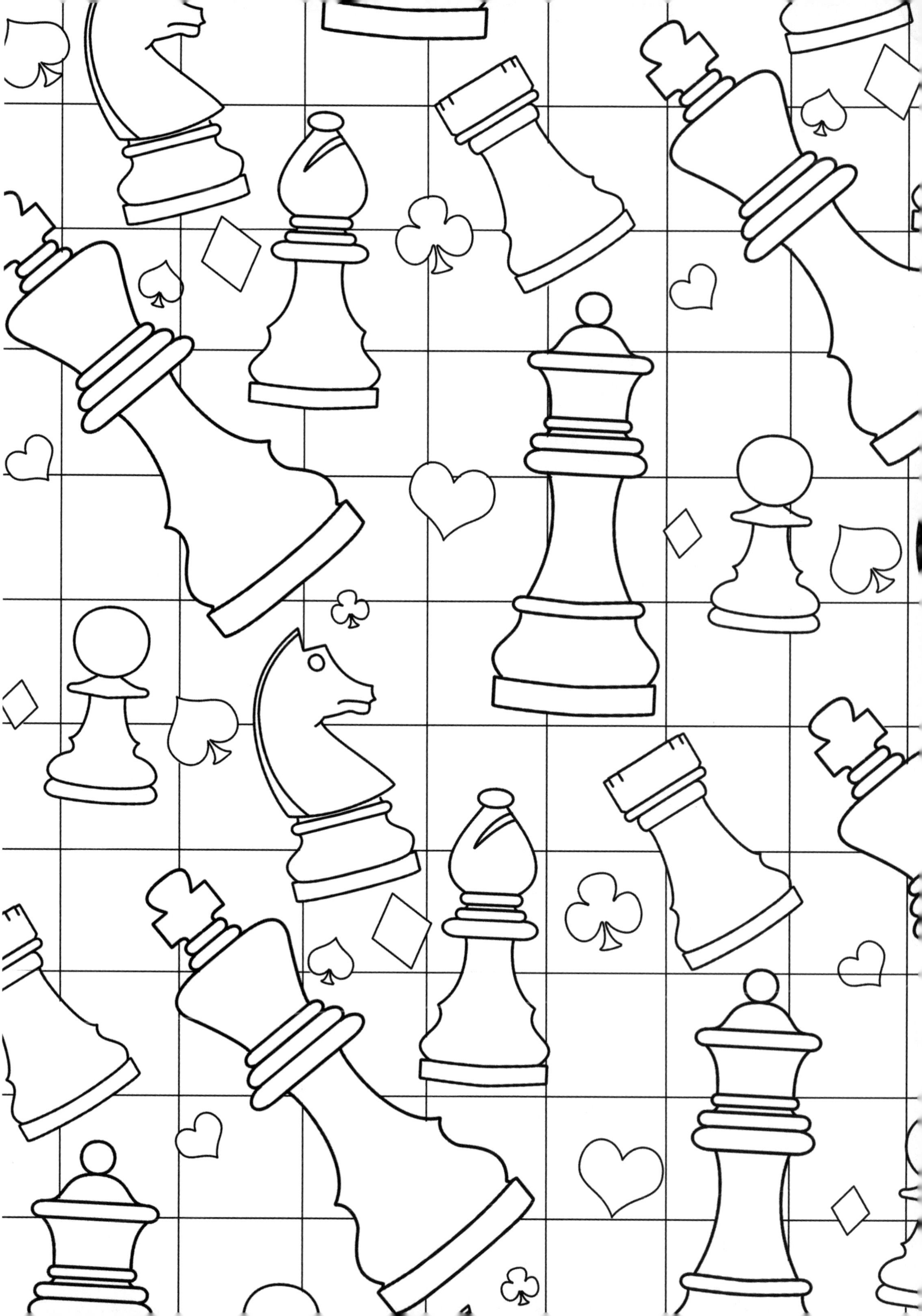

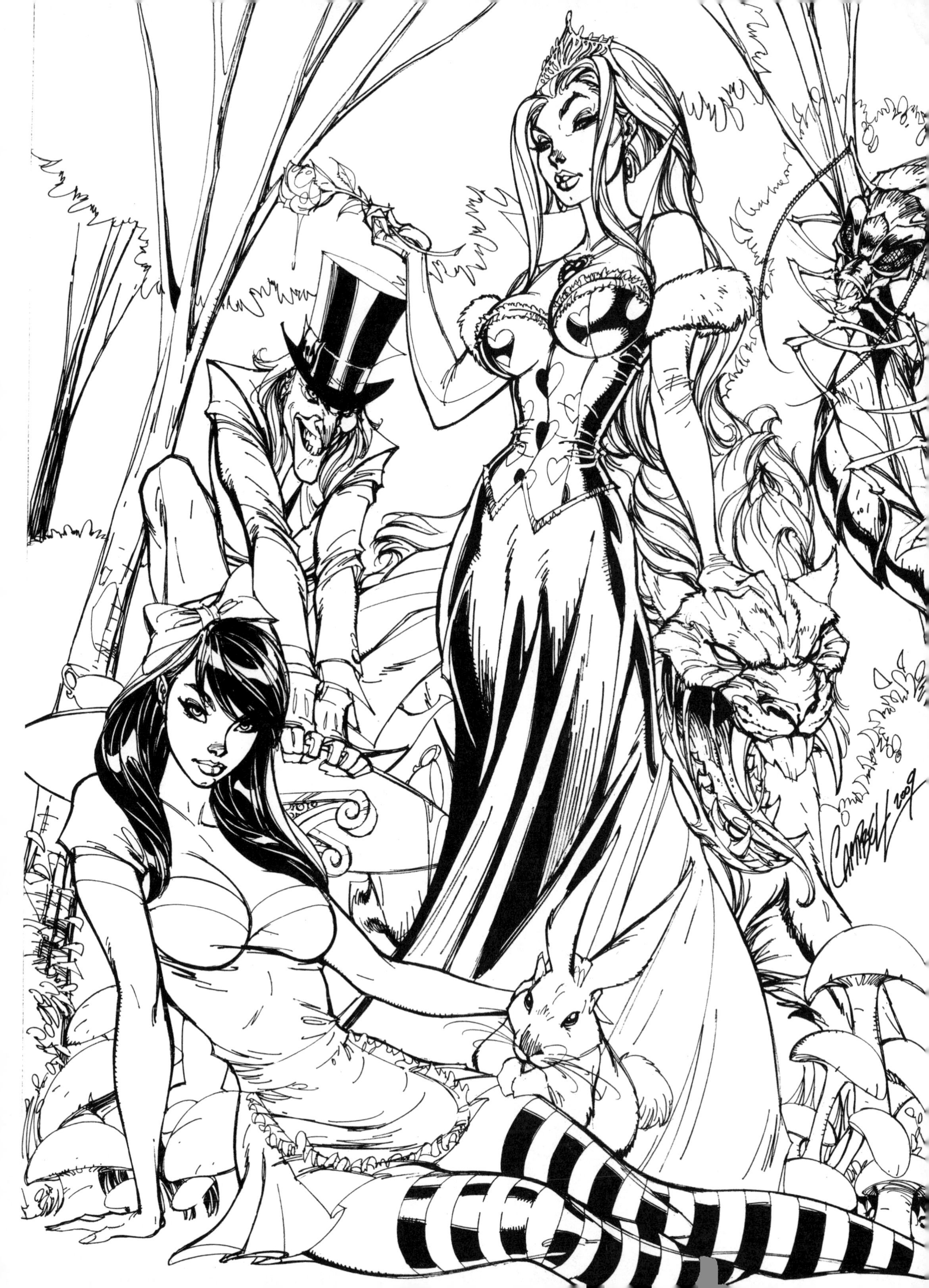

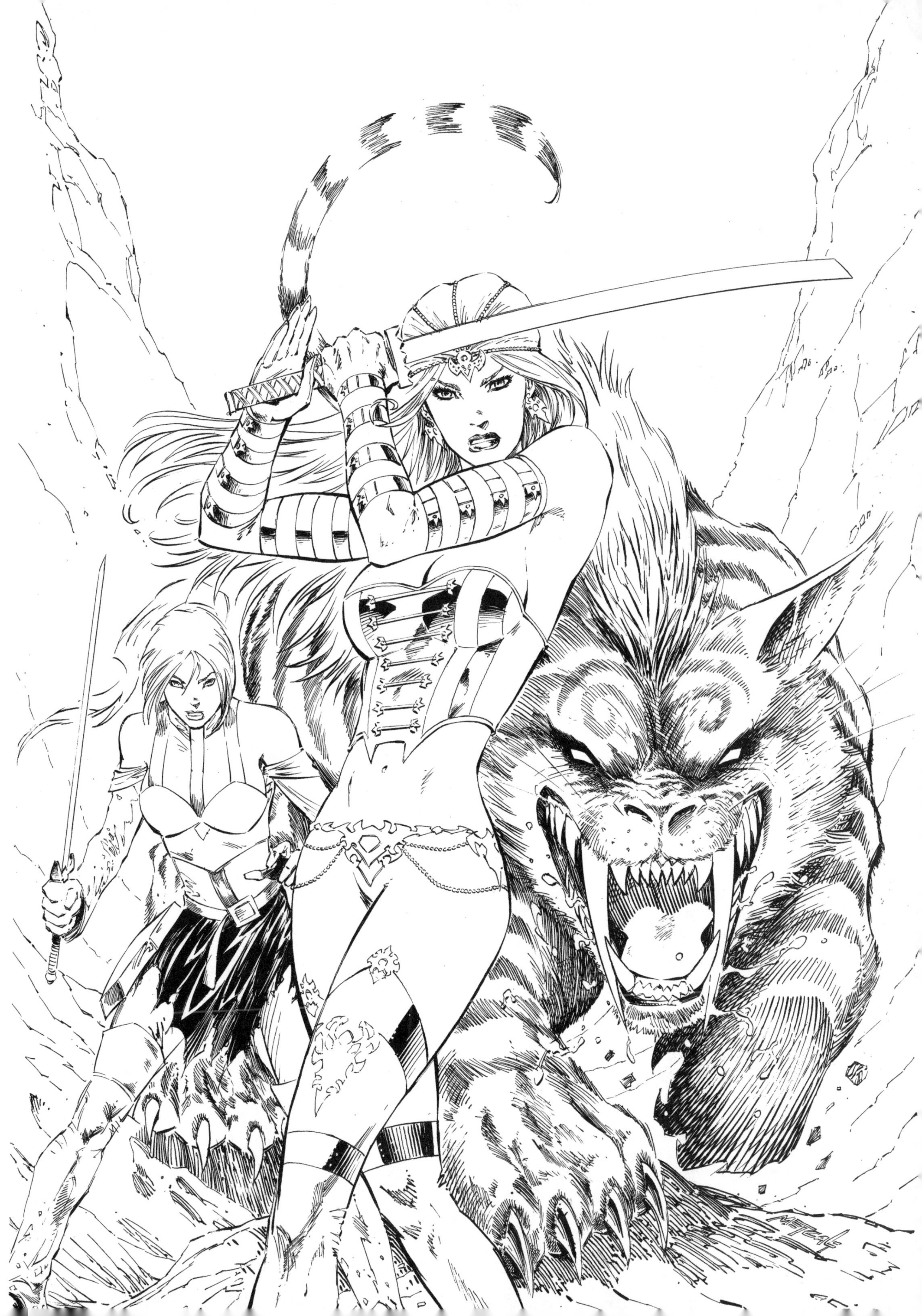

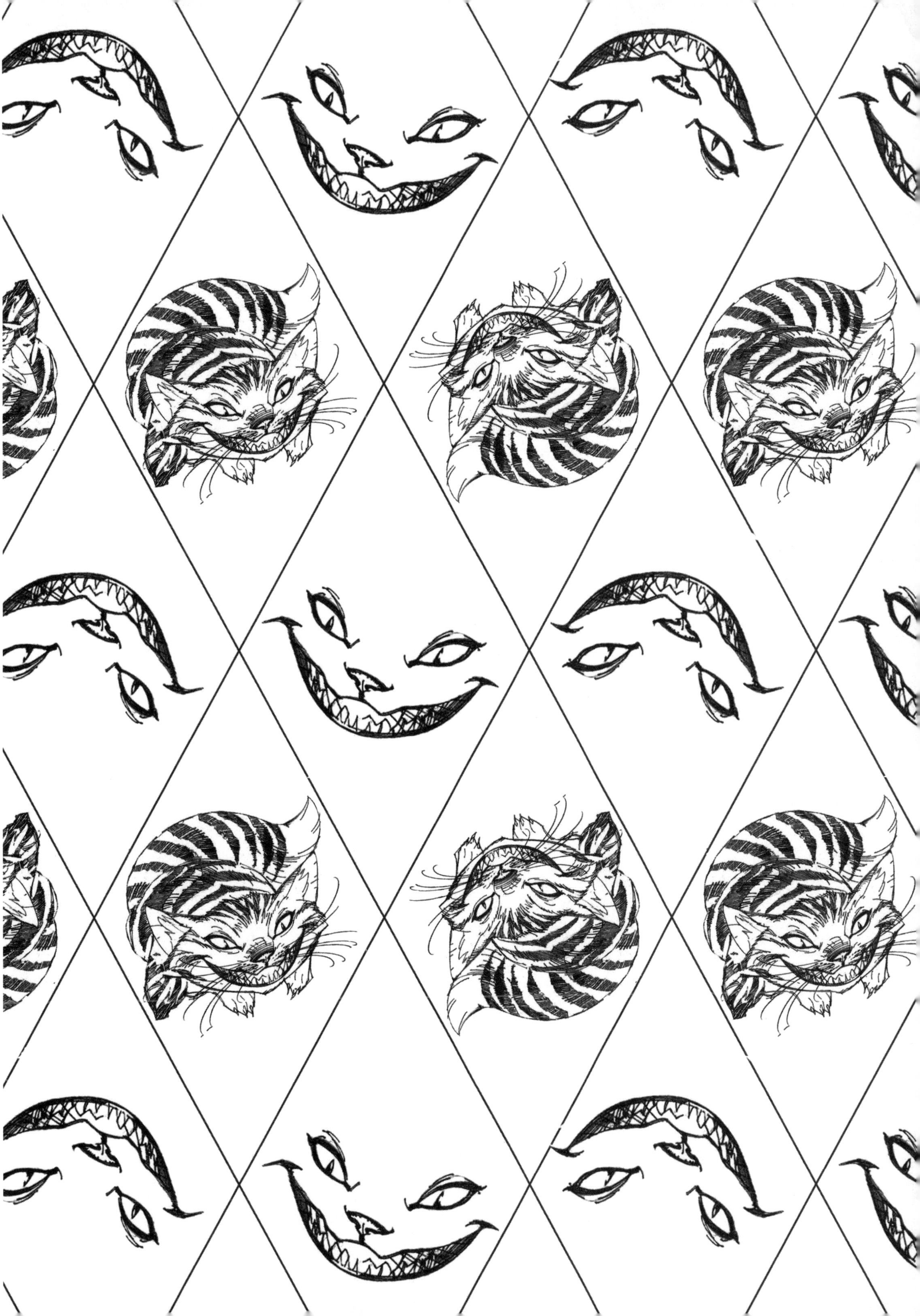

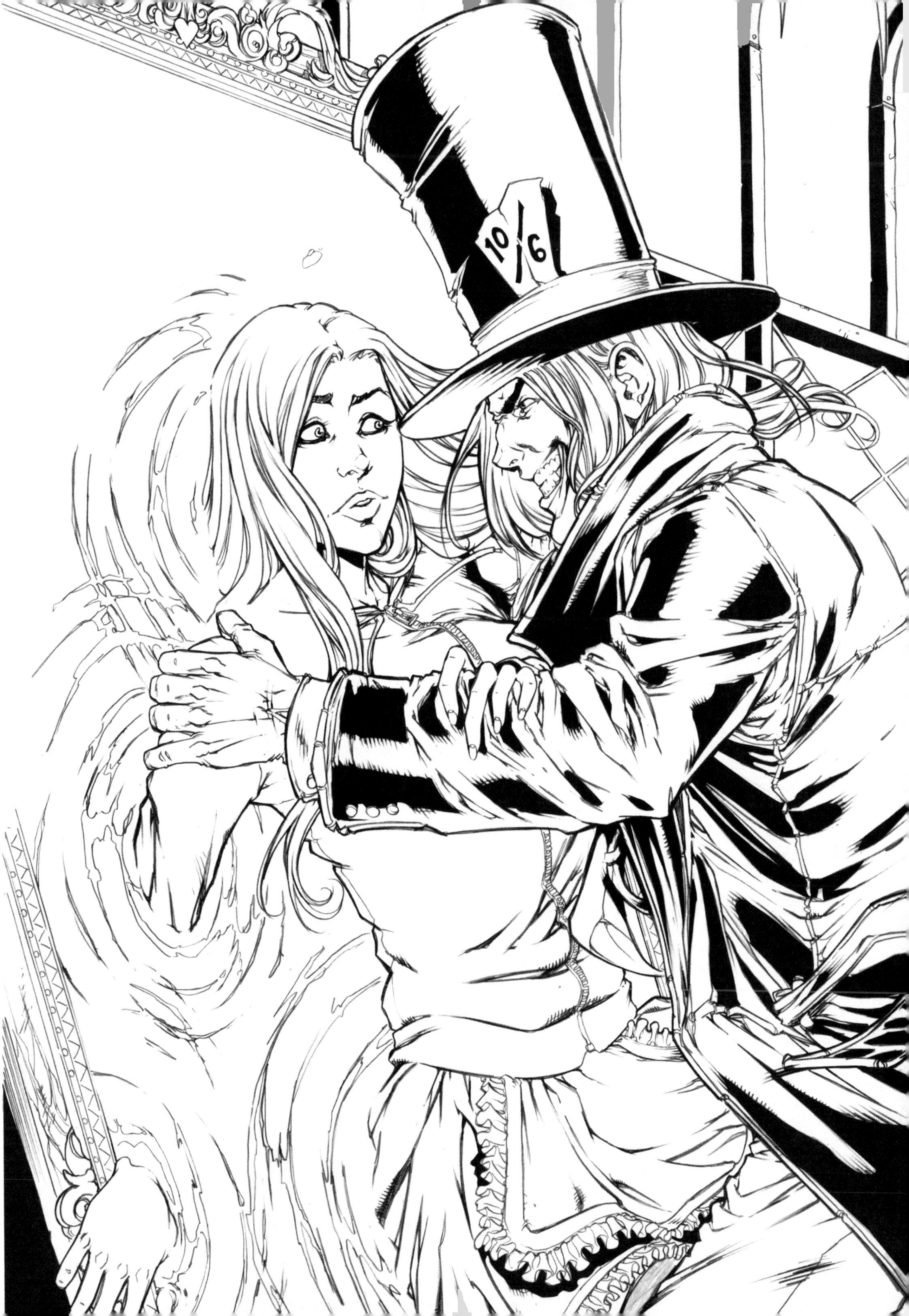
10/6

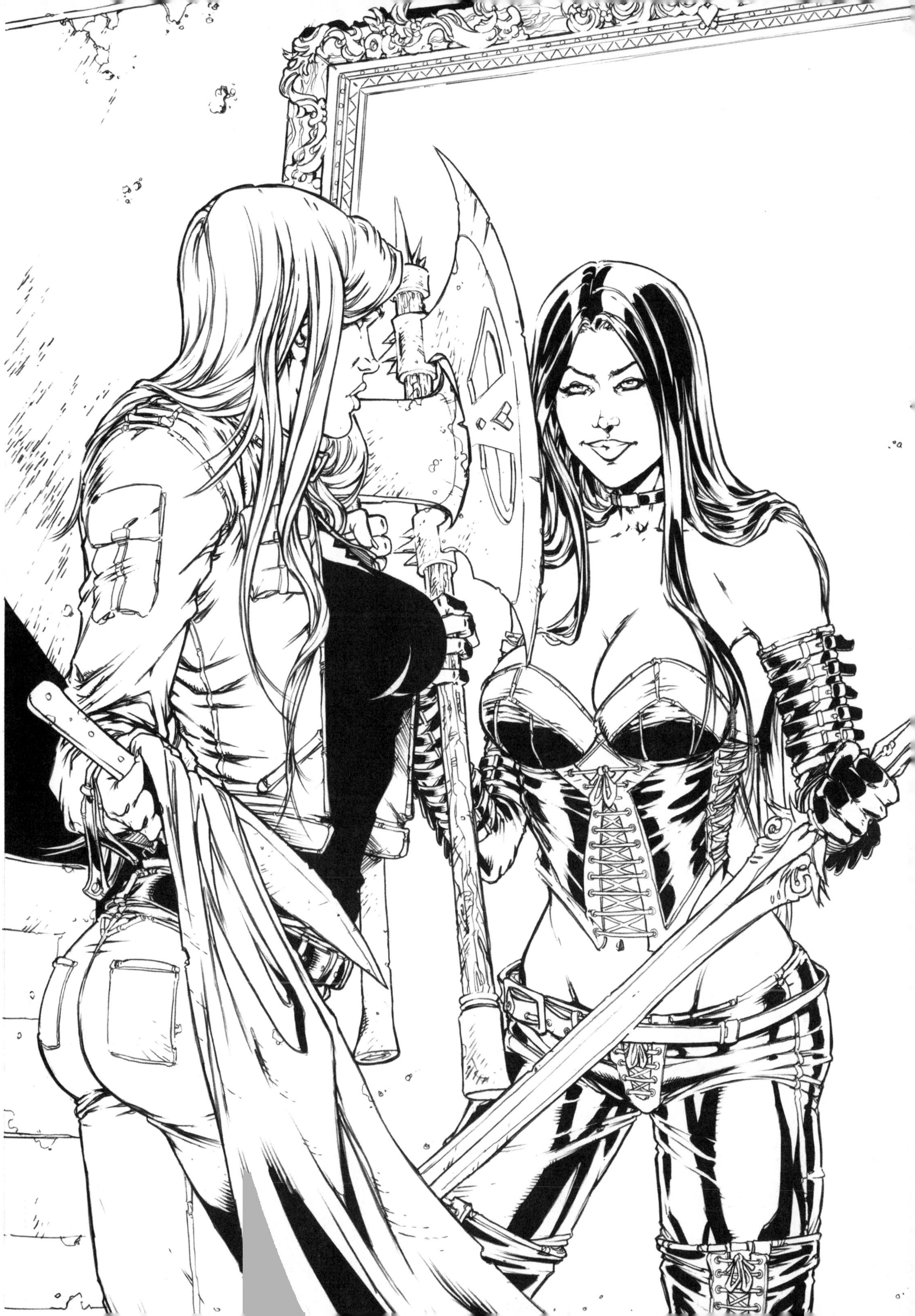

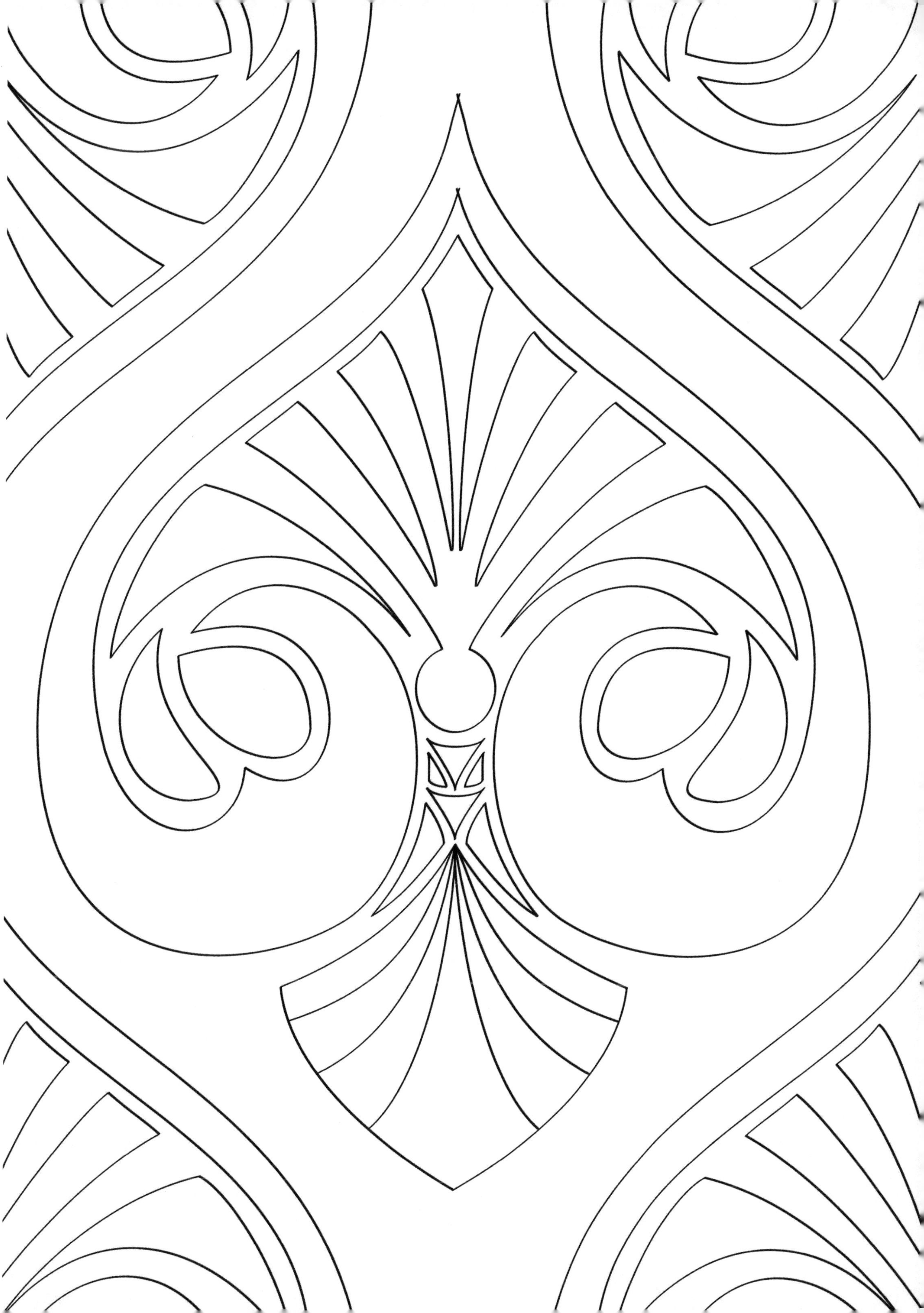

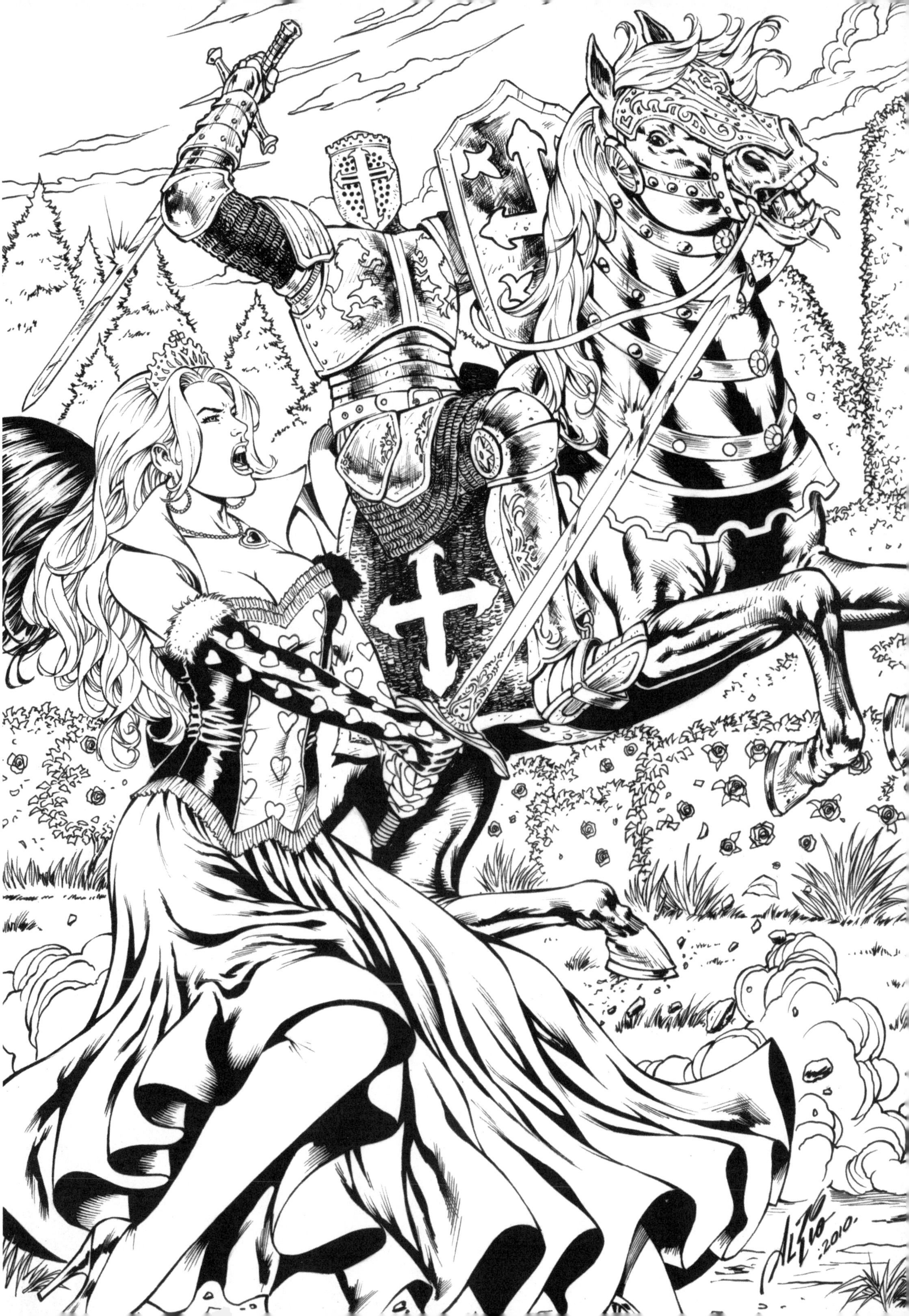
2010

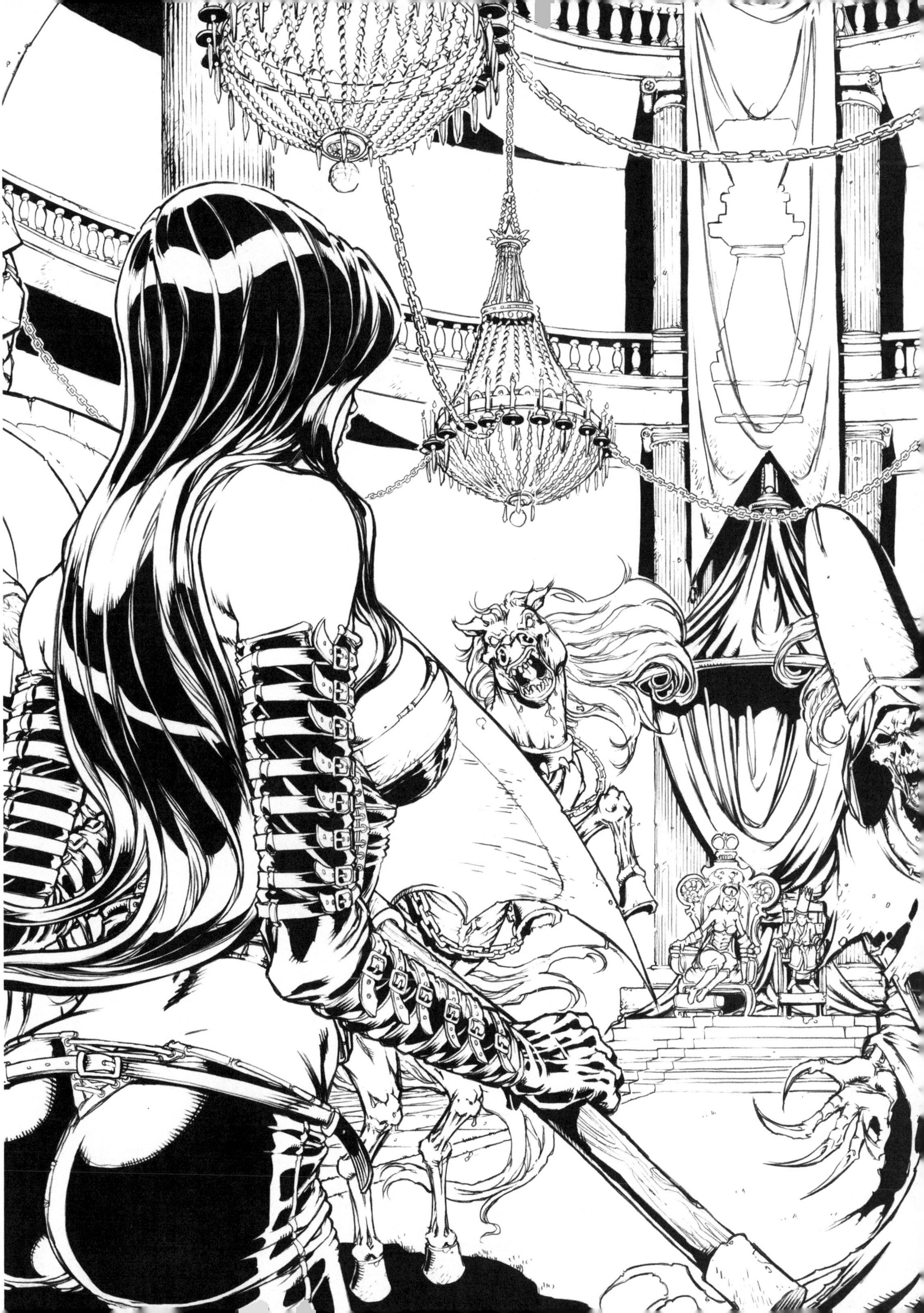

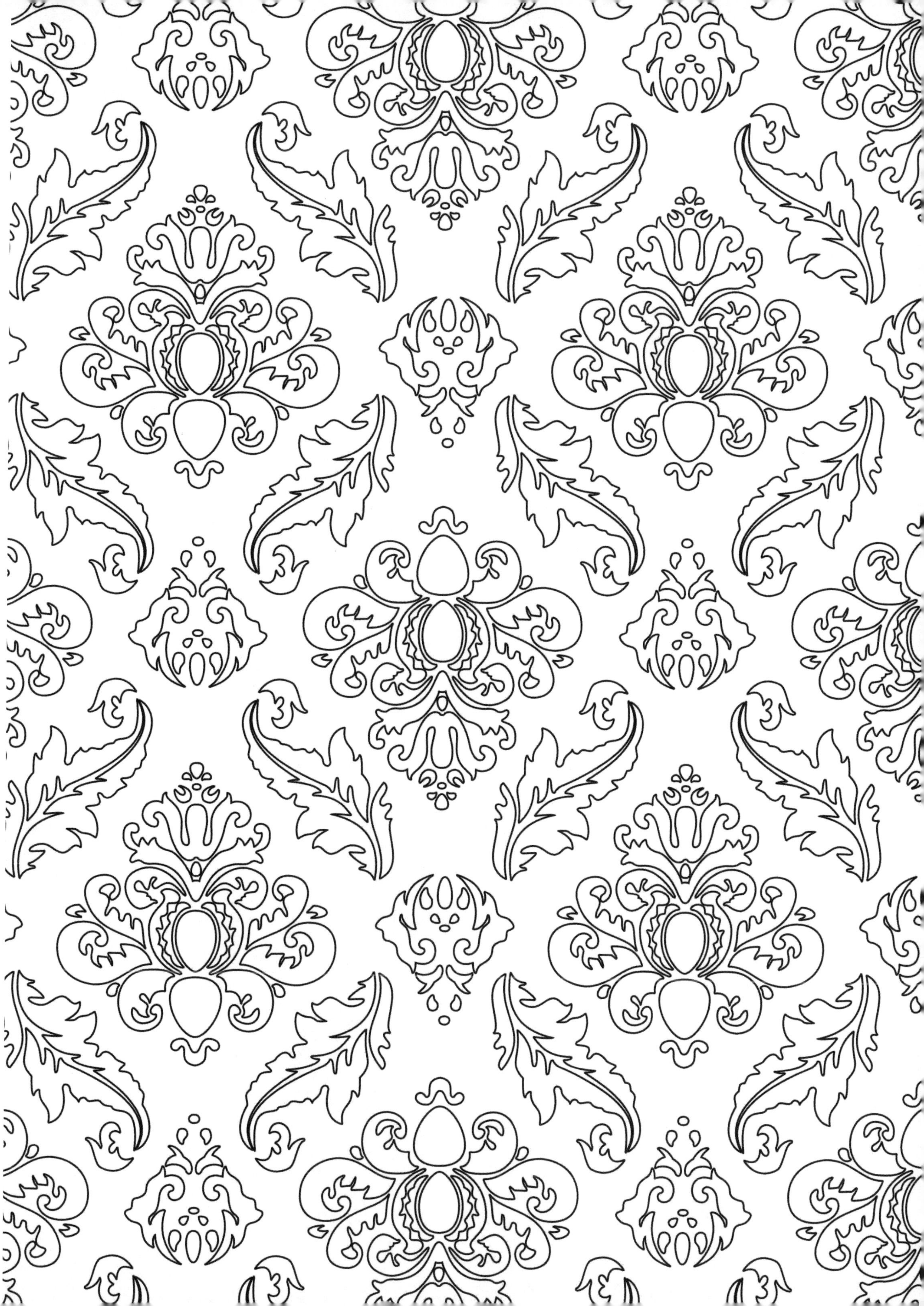

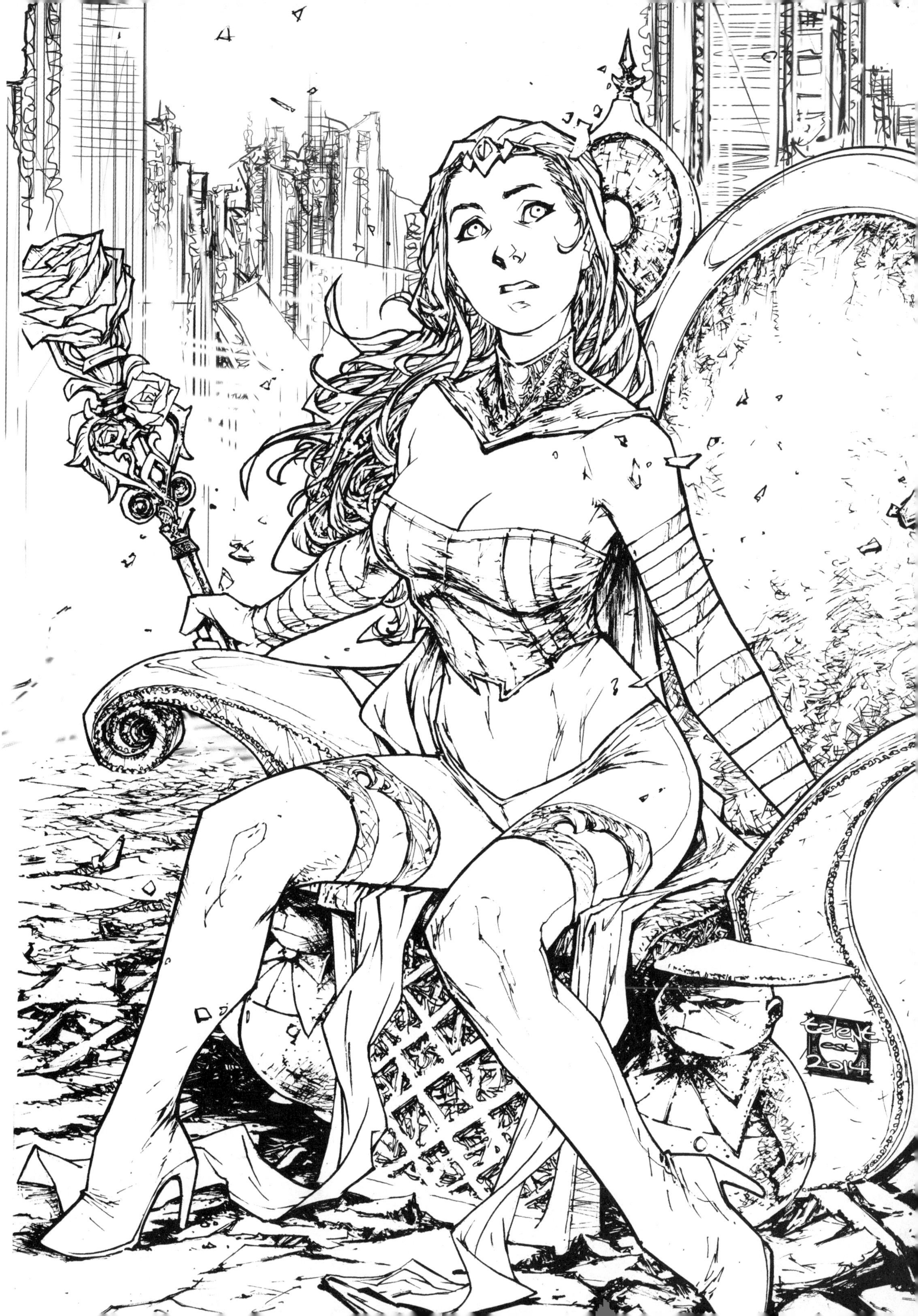
talent
est
2014

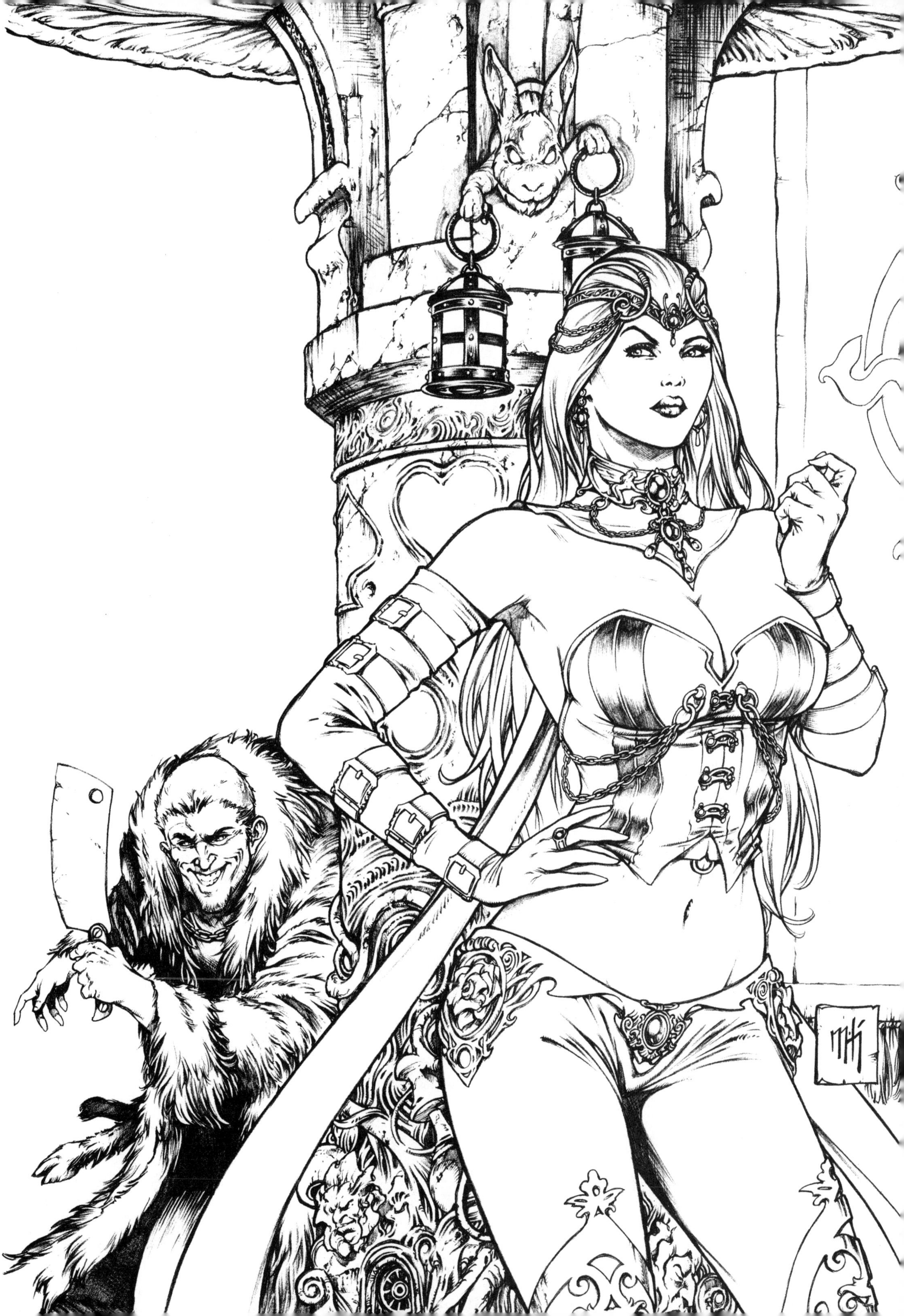

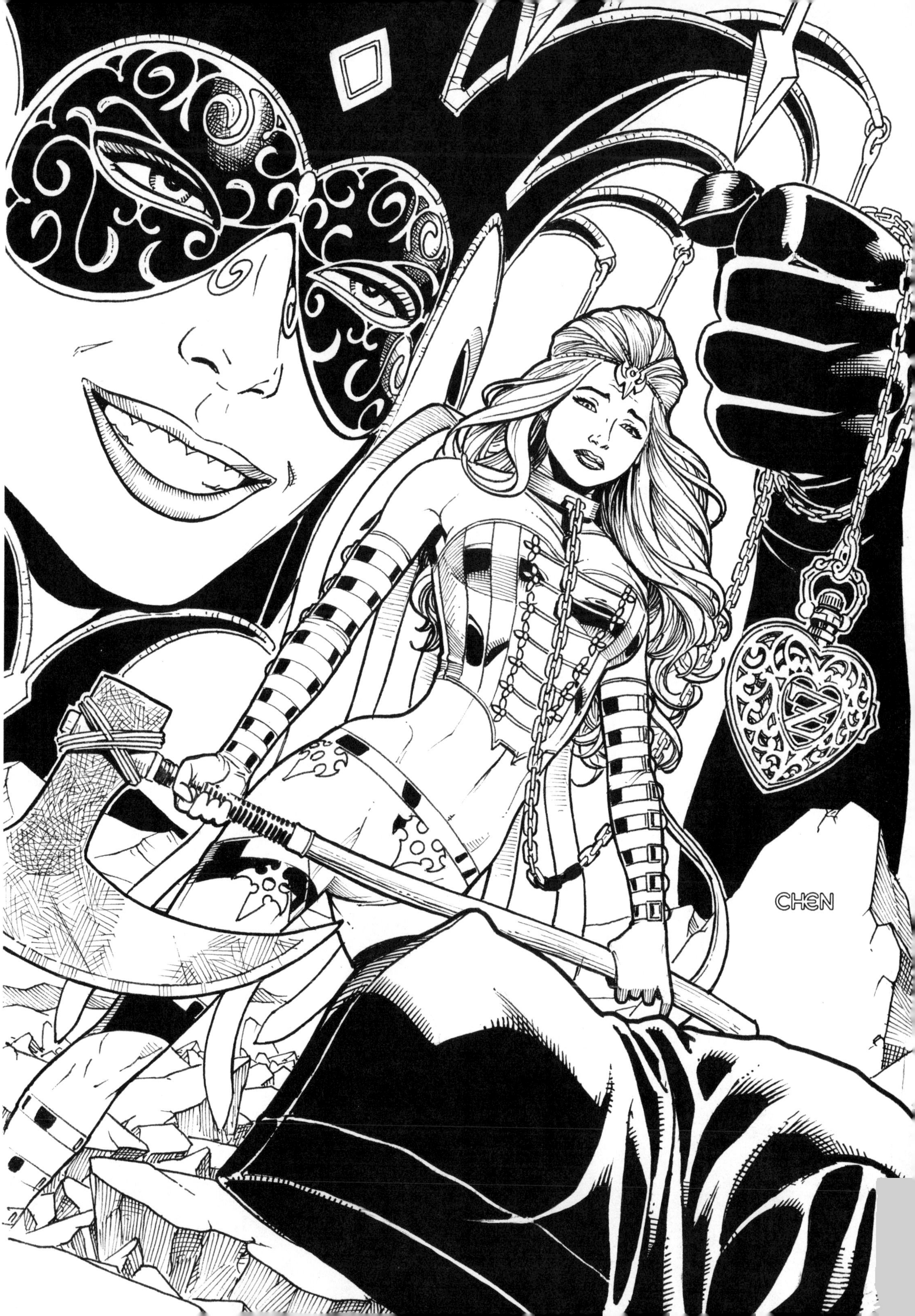
CHEN

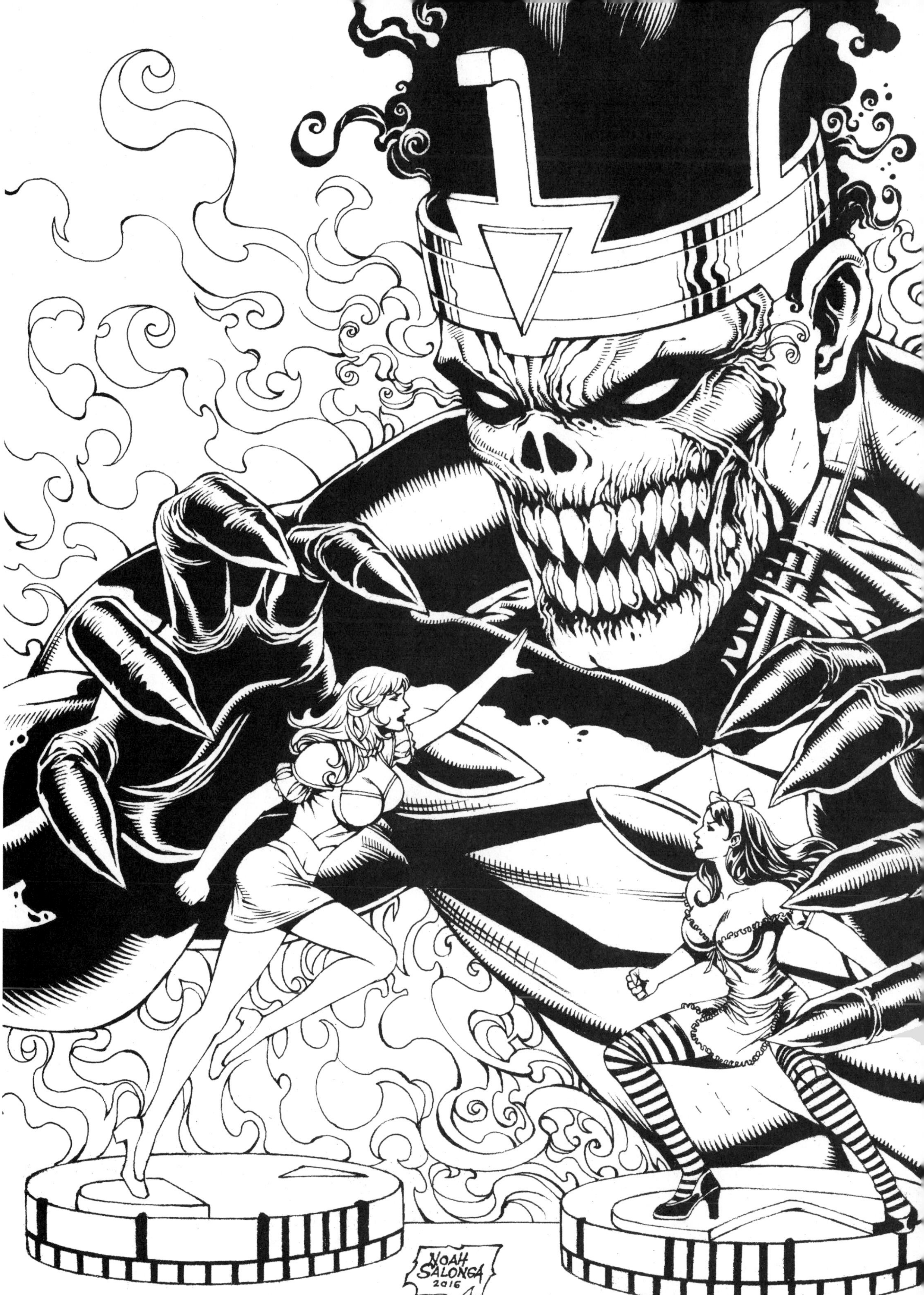
NOAH SALONGA 2016

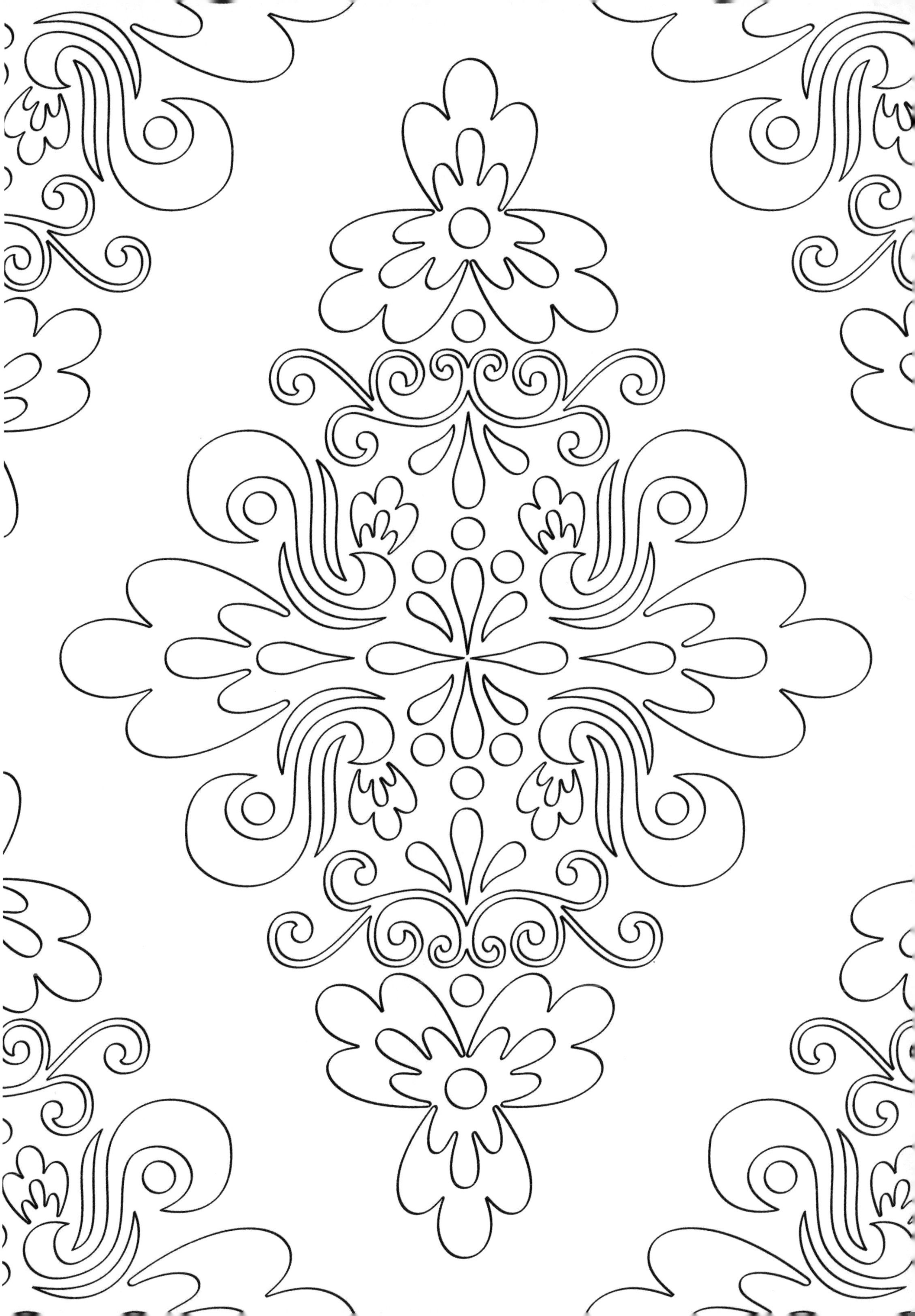

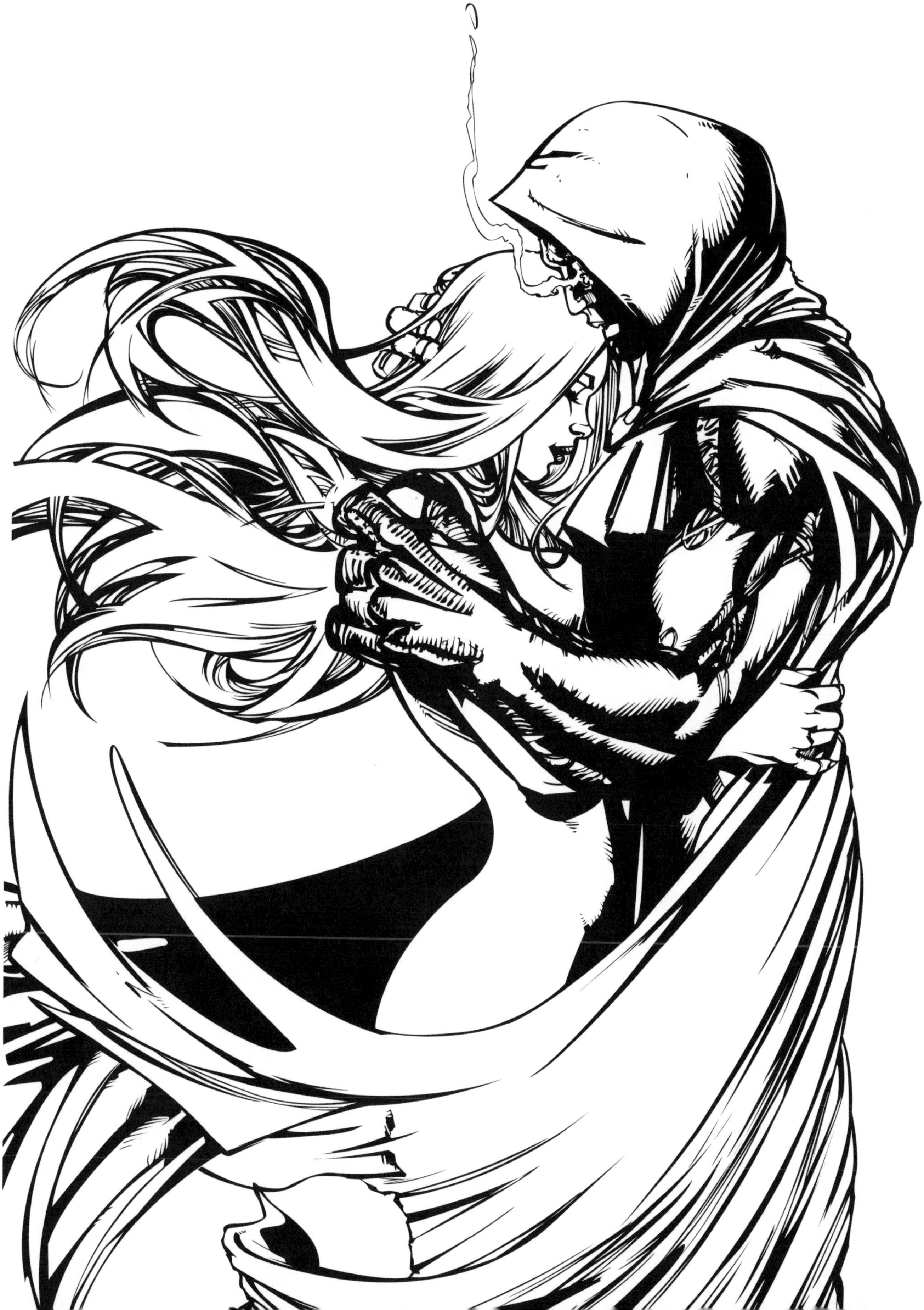

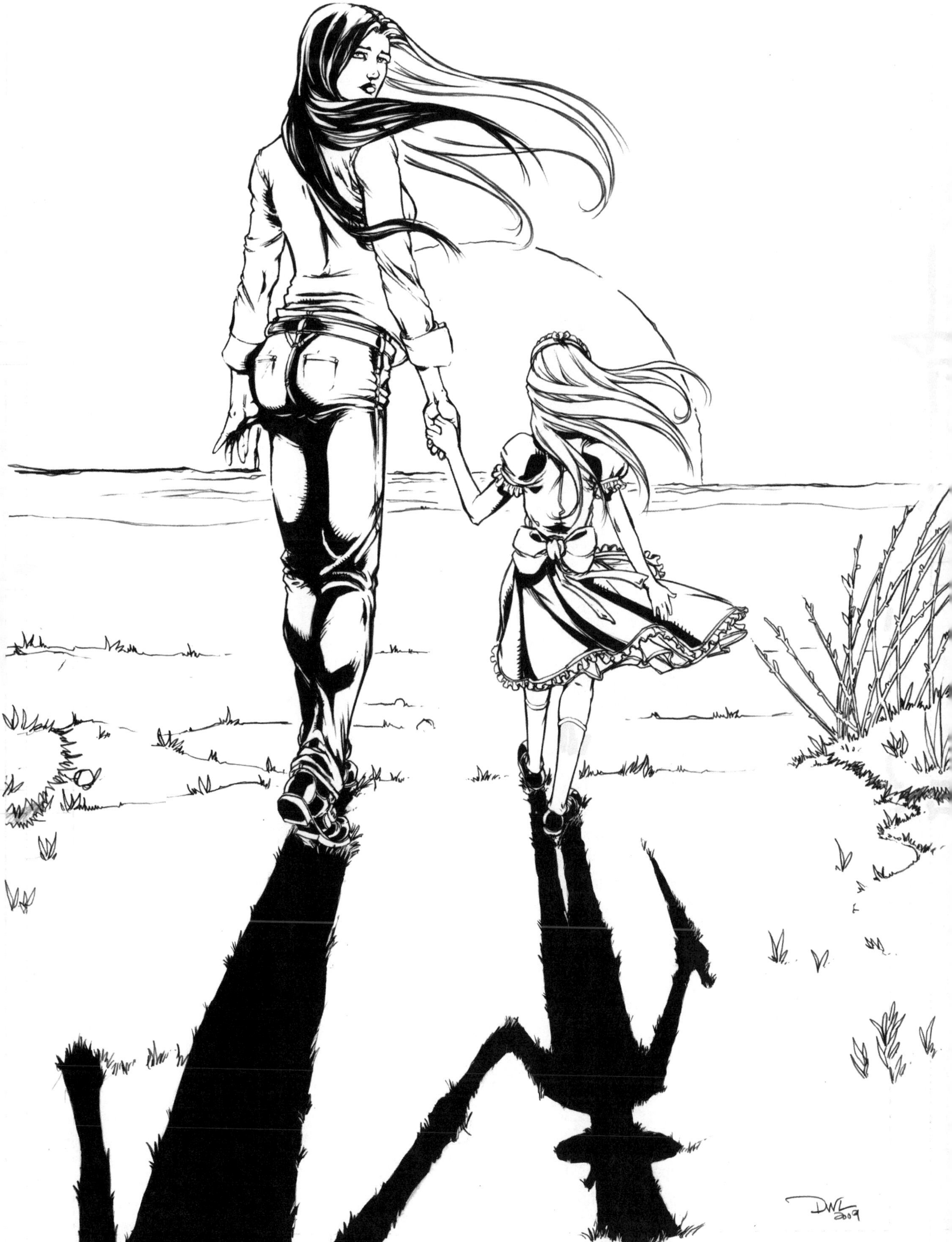
DWL
2009

WE'RE ALL MAD HERE AT ZENESCOPE!

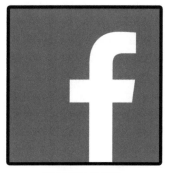

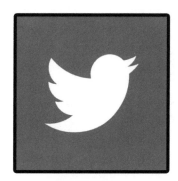

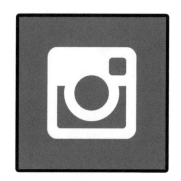

FACEBOOK:
ZENESCOPE
ENTERTAINMENT

TWITTER:
@ZENESCOPE

INSTAGRAM:
@ZENESCOPE

SHARE YOUR COLORING SKILLS WITH US!

#ZENESCOPE

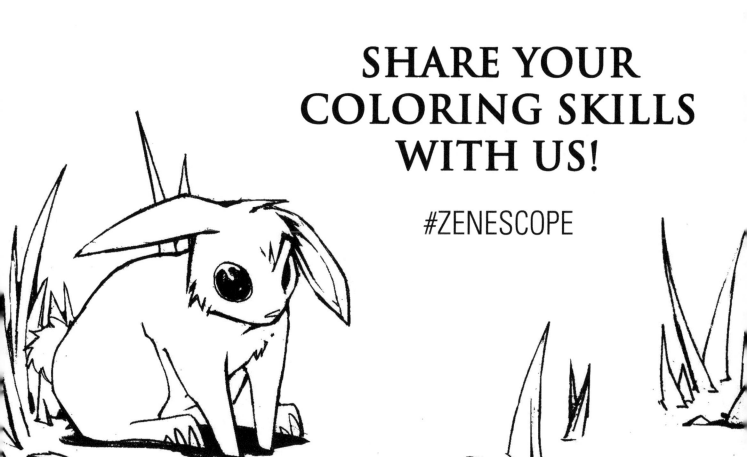

CONTINUE THE CREATIVITY WITH MORE ZENESCOPE COLORING BOOKS

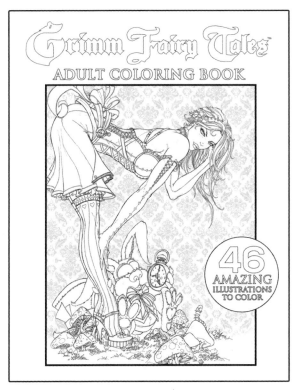

Grimm Fairy Tales™
ADULT COLORING BOOK
46
AMAZING
ILLUSTRATIONS
TO COLOR

NOW AVAILABLE

Grimm Fairy Tales™
ADULT COLORING BOOK

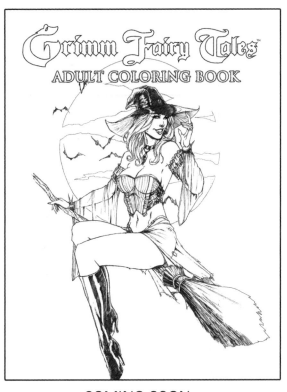

COMING SOON

IF YOU LOVE THE ARTWORK, TRY THE GRAPHIC NOVELS!

Grimm Fairy Tales
Return to Wonderland
Raven Gregory
Daniel Leister
Nei Ruffino

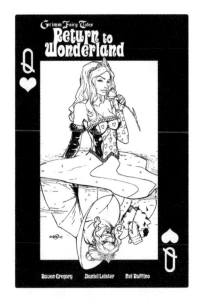

RETURN TO WONDERLAND
BOOK 1

Grimm Fairy Tales
Raven Gregory
Daniel Leister
Nei Ruffino
Beyond Wonderland

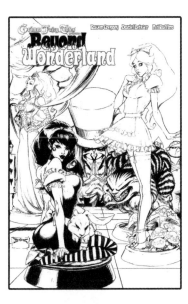

BEYOND WONDERLAND
BOOK 2

Escape from Wonderland
Raven Gregory
Daniel Leister
Nei Ruffino

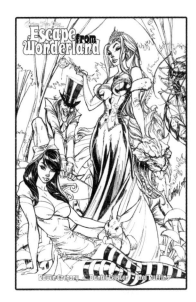

ESCAPE FROM WONDERLAND
BOOK 3